Foundation Sanskrit

Second Edition

David Hodgkinson

Originals
Delhi-110052

Distributed By:
D K Publishers Distributors P Ltd.
4834/24, Ansari Road, Darya Ganj,
New Delhi-110002
Phones: 3278368, 3261465
Fax : 3264368
visit us at: www.dkpd.com
e-mail: dkpd@del3.vsnl.net.in

First Published 1997
Second Edition 2000

ISBN 81-7536-217-0

Published By:
ORIGINALS
(an imprint of Low Price Publications)
A-6, Nimri Commercial Centre,
Near Ashok Vihar Phase-IV,
Delhi-110052
Phone: 7401672, 7452453
visit us at: www.lppindia.com
e-mail: lpp@nde.vsnl.net.in

Printed At:
D K Fine Art Press P Ltd.
Delhi-110052

PRINTED IN INDIA

The Perfect Prayer

ॐ पूर्णमदः पूर्णमिदं पूर्णात्पूर्णमुदच्यते।
पूर्णस्य पूर्णमादाय पूर्णमेवावशिष्यते॥
ॐ शान्तिः शान्तिः शान्तिः॥

That is perfect. This is perfect.
Perfect comes from perfect.
Take perfect from perfect, the remainder is perfect.
May Peace and Peace and Peace
Be everywhere.

Acknowledgements

I would like to acknowledge the support of the Indian Embassy in Dublin, without whose generosity the first draft of this book would not have been printed. The support and encouragement of the teachers of St James School in London, and the work by Mr Nicholas Kazanas of Athens, Dr Stephen Thompson and Mr Brian Hodgkinson, who read the text at various stages in its production, have greatly improved this course. The new verse translation of the Gītā by Mr Brian Hodgkinson is a most welcome addition to the text, for which thanks are due. Thanks are also due to Mr Arthur Farndell for his proof-reading of the second edition, and Mrs Miriam Stollar for her careful commentary on the text after teaching it at St James Boys' School in London.

Introduction

Sanskrit is one of the richest languages of the world. It not only gives access to a wealth of knowledge and wisdom which remains to a large extent undiscovered by the West, but also its grammar as formulated by the grammarian Pāṇini is a masterpiece, unique in the study of language for its precision, clarity and brevity. The literature and philosophy composed in this language have a beauty and profundity, which is unsurpassed.

The *Foundation Sanskrit* course is intended for anyone over the age of ten who wishes to begin a study of the language. An ability to read and write the Sanskrit script is assumed, although a brief summary of the Devanāgarī script has been included. The grammatical aspect of the language is introduced *padam padam*, step by step. There are eighteen chapters. Each introduces a grammatical principle with the help of a story. The emphasis is on understanding these principles. Therefore, only a few words are given at the beginning of each chapter for the student to learn. This enables students to grasp the grammar and learn thoroughly whatever vocabulary is needed. There are plenty of exercises to reinforce the grammatical point. The appendices at the back summarise the material to be learnt in the course: Grammar, Syntax and Vocabulary.

Some scripture is included at the beginning of this course. This is only intended by way of example. It is hoped that teachers will supplement it to their own taste. This is an aspect of the course which cannot be prescribed: it is hoped that students and teachers will take a little time to study something original which they find of value. The stories are also intended to present some aspects of the philosophical tradition which is expressed in the language. They are written in a simple way so that both children and adults may enjoy some of the philosophical lessons of this tradition.

The principles need to be learnt by heart. In teaching and studying this course always move carefully and thoroughly, never rushing a point. Revision and recitation at every stage with regular testing is essential. It is more profitable to move steadily and thoroughly than in leaps and bounds which will leave gaps at a later stage. These are the foundations of the language and without a thorough knowledge of them further progress will be hindered.

The Sanskrit Grammatical Terms as laid down by the Grammarian Pāṇini have been used in the course, wherever appropriate. His system of Vibhakti or Cases forms the basis of Part One of the course. Hence his ordering has been adopted rather than the system used in the West. In the second edition, however, the Western Latin based words for the Cases have been included in the text. These are not intended as a substitute for the Sanskrit terms, but rather to make clear that while the names and systems of the East and West may differ, the underlying concepts are the same. When the student comes to the study of Pāṇini's own sūtras, this early introduction will help to clear the way for swift progress.

Sandhi has not been included in this course, so that the student may make some progress with the reading of the language, and gain some enjoyment from the stories. This inevitably means that some aspects of the study are not fully treated, such as the development of words from their roots, but these will be studied in detail in a later volume, when the student has gained some interest in the language. More mature students and teachers would profit greatly from a study of the words contained in the course, using a dictionary.

Since the course was first produced in 1997, various teachers and students have generously commented on the text. The changes made since then are substantial, and it is hoped that they will clarify points which were previously unclear. The story in Chapter 13 has also been completely rewritten to replace the previous, somewhat unsatisfactory, composition. At various other points the stories and exercises have been improved and the text made a little more thorough-going.

David L.S. Hodgkinson,
July 2000

Table of Contents

Part 1:
Chapters 1-9

THE SANSKRIT ALPHABET

ॐ

अ इ ऋ ऌ उ

क च ट त प

ख छ ठ थ फ

ग ज ड द ब

घ झ ढ ध भ

ङ ञ ण न म

ह य र ल व

श ष स

GUIDE TO SANSKRIT PRONUNCIATION

The following is intended merely to give a brief summary of the Alphabet to help students on their way. It is impossible to write the sounds of one language in another, as they are special to that language. Anyone, therefore, who wishes to learn this language thoroughly is encouraged to see what follows merely as an *aide-mémoire* and to seek guidance from someone who can take him or her through the pronunciation.

Vowels

अ	आ	इ	ई	उ	ऊ	ऋ	ॠ	ऌ	ए	ओ	ऐ	औ
a	ā	i	ī	u	ū	ṛ	ṝ	ḷ	e	o	ai	au

When vowels are written in conjunction with consonants, the following symbols are used:

ा	ि	ी	ु	ू	ृ	ॄ	े	ो	ै	ौ
ā	i	ī	u	ū	ṛ	ṝ	e	o	ai	au

Consonants

The consonants are divided by their mouth positions. The full table of the Sanskrit Alphabet is laid out according to these families in columns, with a vowel at the head of each (see previous page). In each case the symbol as written includes the vowel अ. A ् symbol is used to indicate the absence of any vowel for example, क् = k.

1. In the Throat, कण्ठ्य

क	ख	ग	घ	ङ	ह
ka	kha	ga	gha	ña	ha

2. In the Palate, तालव्य

च	छ	ज	झ	ञ	य	श
ca	cha	ja	jha	ña	ya	śa

3. In the Roof of the Mouth, मूर्धन्य

ट	ठ	ड	ढ	ण	र	ष
ṭa	ṭha	ḍa	ḍha	ṇa	ra	ṣa

4. On the Teeth, दन्त्य

त	थ	द	ध	न	ल	स
ta	tha	da	dha	na	la	sa

5. On the Lips, ओष्ठ्य

प	फ	ब	भ	म	व
pa	pha	ba	bha	ma	va

Consonants in combination with one another frequently lose the vertical line which indicates an अ (when no other vowel is written).

1. In the throat, कण्ठ्य

क्	ख्	ग्	घ्	ङ्	ह्*
k	kh	g	gh	ṅ	h

* There are various combinations of ह which are not listed here, but, in the main, are clear enough when seen.
The following may, however, cause some confusion:

क्र = kra

क्ष = kṣa

क्त = kta

2. In the Palate, तालव्य

च्	छ्	ज्	झ्	ञ्	य्	श्
c	ch	j	jh	ñ	y	ś

The symbol ज्ञ = jña.

3. In the Roof of the Mouth, मूर्धन्य

ट्	ठ्	ड्	ढ्	ण्	र्	ष्
ṭ	ṭh	ḍ	ḍh	ṇ	r	ṣ

4. On the Teeth, दन्त्य

त्	थ्	द्	ध्	न्	ल्	स्
t	th	d	dh	n	l	s

A Double त is त्त. The symbol त्र is a 'tra'.

5. On the Lips, ओष्ठ्य

प्	फ्	ब्	भ्	म्	व्
p	ph	b	bh	m	v

The symbol प्र = 'pra'.

Note that the above list is by no means exhaustive. Many others, however, can be 'worked out' from what is given here.

The विसर्ग

The two dots (:) often placed at the end of a word indicate a विसर्ग or slight breath after the preceeding sound. In English script a विसर्ग is written ḥ.

The अनुस्वार

An अनुस्वार is written as a dot above a letter and indicates a nasal sound after that letter. For example, सिंह = siṁha (This will be explained further in the *Intermediate Sanskrit* Course)

Reading Practice

The माहेश्वराणि सूत्राणि form a starting point for much of the system of Sanskrit Grammar laid down by Pāṇini. He uses them to identify groups of sounds. In this course they will not be used until the later stages. They are included here as a simple exercise to practise reading and recitation.

॥ अथ माहेश्वराणि सूत्राणि ॥

अइउण्। ऋऌक्। एओङ्। ऐऔच्।

हयवरट्। लण्। ञमङणनम्। झभञ्।

घढधष्। जबगडदश्। खफछठथचटतव्।

कपय्। शषसर्। हल्।

॥ इति माहेश्वराणि सूत्राणि ॥

SCRIPTURE

श्रीभगवानुवाच।

अभयम् सत्त्वसंशुद्धिर्ज्ञानयोगव्यवस्थितिः।
दानं दमश्च यज्ञश्च स्वाध्यायस्तप आर्जवम् ॥१॥
अहिंसा सत्यमक्रोधस्त्यागः शान्तिरपैशुनम् ।
दया भूतेष्वलोलुप्त्वं मार्दवं ह्रीरचापलम् ॥२॥
तेजः क्षमा धृतिः शौचमद्रोहो नातिमानिता ।
भवन्ति सम्पदं दैवीमभिजातस्य भारत ॥३॥
दम्भो दर्पोऽभिमानश्च क्रोधः पारुष्यमेव च ।
अज्ञानं चाभिजातस्य पार्थ सम्पदमासुरीम् ॥४॥
दैवी सम्पद्विमोक्षाय निबन्धायासुरी मता ।
मा शुचः सम्पदं दैवीमभिजातोऽसि पाण्डव ॥५॥

Then said the Blessed Lord to Arjuna: 1
"Lack of all fear, the purity of mind,
A firm resolve to follow *yoga's* path,
Giving of alms, and worship, self-control,
The study of the scriptures, honesty,
Austerity and absence of all harm, 2
A love of truth, renouncing of desire,
Freedom from anger and all calumny,
Serenity, compassion for all creatures
Of the world, restraint in sense perception,
No useless movement of the tongue or limbs,
Gentleness and modesty to all,
Boldness in action, patience, fortitude, 3
Cleanliness of body and of mind,
The absence of all hatred and of pride:
These are the marks, O son of Bharata,
Of men, whose nature is, by birth, divine.
Whilst arrogance, hypocrisy, conceit, 4
Coarse language, anger, ignorance of truth,
Are signs, O Pārtha, of demonic birth.
The godly state engenders one result: 5
The liberation of those men so born;
Whilst those are bound who are demonic.
Grieve not, O Pāṇḍava, for you were born,
As one of godly nature.

(*Bhagavad Gītā*, Chapter XVI, vv.1-5)

1. THE MAN AND THE BIRD

I. *Vocabulary:*

(Note: students are expected to learn the words given at the beginning of each chapter, but not those given as Notes to the stories.)

वदति	he says
पतति	he falls; flies
चरति	he walks
पश्यति	he sees
तुदति	he hits; strikes; pushes
भवति	he becomes
अचिरेण	soon

II. *Grammar*:

1. A useful starting point for the study of Sanskrit is the धातु.

Definition of धातु

> A धातु is the root form of a word.
> It expresses an action.

For example, the धातु भू indicates 'becoming', while वद् indicates 'speaking'. This gives a stem which can lead to many other words, all connected with speaking, like वदति. When endings are added to a धातु either a Verb or a Noun can be formed. Further endings develop the meaning of words within a sentence. This course looks at how some of these endings function to allow sentences to be produced.

Definition of Number

Singular means one person or thing, Dual means two people or things, and Plural means many people or things.

The Sanskrit word for Number in Grammar is वचन. Hence the words for Singular, Dual and Plural are as follows:

Singular	एकवचन
Dual	द्विवचन
Plural	बहुवचन

Definition of the Three Persons

In English Grammar we speak of the 'Three Persons'.

The First Person is "I" or "we"; the Second Person is "you"; the Final Person is "he, she, it, they" or any name or Noun.

Sanskrit Grammarians used different names for the different Persons. These terms will be used in the course, and the Verbs will be presented in their traditional order, with the 'Third Person' first. The Sanskrit Terms are as follows:

Western Term	Sanskrit Term	Meaning of Sanskrit
Third Person	प्रथमपुरुष	First Person
Second Person	मध्यमपुरुष	Middle Person
First Person	उत्तमपुरुष	Last Person

Note that in the Western 'he, she or it' is called the 'Third Person', but in the Sanskrit system it is called the 'First Person'

2. Note that in all the vocabularies at the beginning of each chapter, the words are listed with the प्रथमपुरुष ending. In English this is indicated by the word 'he', which stands for any one of the meanings of this ending.

When translating a Noun and a Verb together remember not to write 'he' etc.
For example,

रामः भवति means 'Rāma becomes'

NOT 'Rāma he becomes'.

3. Learn to recite and write out the following chart of the Present of भू. This is used as an example, or paradigm, for the Present of the Verbs which you will meet in the course.

Present of 'becomes'

	एकवचन Singular	द्विवचन Dual	बहुवचन Plural
प्रथमपुरुष	भवति	भवतः	भवन्ति
First Person	he becomes	they two become	they become
मध्यमपुरुष	भवसि	भवथः	भवथ
Middle Person	you become	you two become	you become
उत्तमपुरुष	भवामि	भवावः	भवामः
Last Person	I become	we two become	we become

III. *Punctuation:*

1. In Sanskrit sentences are punctuated very simply. A vertical stroke, or विराम, is used to mark the end of a sentence. Two vertical strokes, a पूर्णविराम, are used to mark the end of a unit like a paragraph.
For example, रामः भवति। Rāma becomes.

2. The word इति is used to mark the end of speech, rather as English uses speech marks.
For example, हे राम इति वदति। "O Rāma," he says.

V. ॥नरः खगः च॥

1.एकदा नरः अस्ति।

2.नरः मूर्खः अस्ति।

3.नित्यम् गुरुम् गच्छति।

4.यत् यत् वदामि तत् तत् कुरु इति गुरुः वदति।

5.नरः तु न किंचित् करोति।

6.नरस्य खगः अस्ति।

7.पञ्जरे वसति।

8.एकदा खगः तम् वदति हे नर। गुरुम् पृच्छ कथम् मुक्तः भविष्यामि इति।

9.नरः गुरुम् गच्छति।

10.गुरुम् वदति मम खगः पृच्छति कथम् मुक्तः भविष्यामि इति।

11.सहसा गुरुः भूमिम् पतति।

12.जनाः कुपिताः भवन्ति।

13.नरः अपधावति।

14.गृहम् गच्छति।

15.खगम् पश्यति।

16.खगम् वदति यदा गुरुम् अवदम् तदा सहसा भूमिम् अपतत्। जनाः कुपिताः अभवन् इति।

17.सहसा खगः भूमिम् पतति।

18.नरः पञ्जरस्य द्वारम् अपावृणोति।

19.सहसा खगः शीघ्रम् उत्पतनम् करोति।

20.यत् यत् गुरुः वदति तत् तत् करोमि। ततः अहम् मुक्तः। यदि तथा करोषि तर्हि मुक्तः अचिरेण भविष्यसि इति।

21.नरः गुरुम् गच्छति।

22.गुरुम् पृच्छति किम् मया कर्तव्यम् इति।

23.सत्यम् ज्ञानम् अनन्तम् ब्रह्म अनुस्मर इति गुरुः वदति।

24.सत्यम् ज्ञानम् अनन्तम् ब्रह्म इति नरः नित्यम् अनुस्मरति।

25.अचिरेण मुक्तः भवति।

<u>Notes</u>

1. एकदा	once
नरः	a man
अस्ति	there is *(translate first)*
2. मूर्खः	a fool
अस्ति	is
3. नित्यम्	always
गुरुम्	to a teacher
गच्छति	goes
4. यत् यत्	whatever
तत् तत्	that
कुरु	do
गुरुः	the teacher
5. तु	but
न किंचित्	nothing
करोति	does
6. नरस्य खगः अस्ति	The man has a bird
7. पञ्जरे	in a cage
वसति	lives
8. तम्	to him
हे नर	O man

गुरुम्	the teacher *(Object)*
पृच्छ	ask
कथम्	how?
मुक्तः	liberated
भविष्यामि	will I become
10. मम खगः पृच्छति	my bird asks
11. सहसा	suddenly
भूमिम्	to the ground
12. जनाः	the people
कुपिताः	angry
13. अपधावति	runs away
14. गृहम्	to his house
15. तत्र	there
खगम्	the bird *(Object)*
16. यदा	when
अवदम्	I spoke (to)
तदा	then
अपतत्	he fell
अभवन्	they became
18. पञ्जरस्य द्वारम्	the door of the cage
अपावृणोति	he opens
19. शीघ्रम्	quickly
उत्पतनम् करोति	jumps
20. यत् यत्	whatever

तत् तत्	that
करोमि	I do
अहम्	I am
मुक्तः	liberated
यदि	if
तथा	likewise
करोषि	you do
तर्हि	then
भविष्यसि	you will become
22. किम् मया कर्तव्यम्	what must I do?
23. सत्यम् ज्ञानम् अनन्तम् ब्रह्म	Brahman is truth, knowledge, infinite
अनुस्मर	remember

Chapter 1 Exercises

Section A

1. *Write out all nine forms of* भवति *and their meanings.*

2. *Write out all nine forms of* वदति *and their meanings.*

Section B

(i) *Write down each of the following words.*
(ii) *Underline the ending, and state who is doing the action.*

1.	चरति	6.	वदसि
2.	भवन्ति	7.	पततः
3.	वदामः	8.	चरावः
4.	तुदामि	9.	पश्यसि
5.	चरन्ति	10.	वदामि

Section C

(i) *Give two English words which come from the* धातु चर्.
(ii) *Say what the action is in each of the following words:*

1.	चरसि	6.	वदसि
2.	भवामि	7.	पतथः
3.	वदावः	8.	चरावः
4.	तुदति	9.	पश्यसि
5.	चरतः	10.	वदामि

Section D

(i) *State (a) the* वचन (Number)

(b) the पुरुष (Person) *of each of the following,*

(ii) *Translate each.*

1. वदति	11. चरसि
2. तुदामि	12. पश्यतः
3. पतन्ति	13. वदथः
4. वदथ	14. पश्यति
5. तुदसि	15. पश्यसि
6. पतामि	16. वदावः
7. पश्यामः	17. चरामि
8. तुदावः	18. पतामः
9. चरंति	19. पश्यन्ति
10. तुदतः	20. चरामः

Section E

Translate the following into Sanskrit:

1. They fall	11. They two fall
2. I hit	12. We two hit
3. They see	13. We see
4. He walks	14. They walk
5. You fall	15. You many fall
6. We two see	16. They two say
7. You see	17. You two speak
8. We two say	18. You two fall
9. They two strike	19. We strike
10. They say	20. I see

2. THE BIRD WHICH STANDS IN THE TREE

I. *Vocabulary*:

Learn the following words, and revise those from chapter 1.

खगः	bird
वृक्षः	tree
नरः	man
सिंहः	lion
गजः	elephant
खादति	he eats
तिष्ठति	he stands
गायति	he sings
हरति	he takes; grabs

II. *Grammar:*

Learn the प्रथमा विभक्ति of राम, with its meanings.

एकवचन	द्विवचन	बहुवचन	
रामः	रामौ	रामाः	प्रथमा विभक्ति
Rāma	two Rāmas	Rāmas	Nominative

III. Syntax:

Introduction to the System of विभक्ति

In Chapter 1, each of the endings given for a क्रिया shows who is doing the action.
The endings of a नाम will now be introduced. Each shows the role of the person or thing in the action. There are seven such roles, each shown by different endings. As there may be one, two or many people playing any role, there are also three different endings for these: एकवचन, द्विवचन and बहुवचन. Therefore in Sanskrit every नाम can take any one of twenty-one different endings. The endings are given in seven groups of three called विभक्ति.

1. The प्रथमा विभक्ति Rule

Learn the following rule by heart.

The प्रथमा विभक्ति Rule
The प्रथमा विभक्ति shows the Subject of a Sentence.

The प्रथमा विभक्ति is called the 'Nominative' by Western Grammarians, because it *names* something (Nominative comes from the Latin *nomen* meaning 'name'.)

For example,

रामः चरति। Rāma walks.

वृक्षः पतति। The tree falls.

2. 'A' and 'The'

Notice that in English we do not say 'Tree falls'. We use the words 'the' or 'a'. There are no such words in Sanskrit. Therefore, the sentence वृक्षः पतति। could mean, "A tree falls.", or "The tree calls".

3. The Vocabularies

In the *Vocabulary* Sections, each Noun will be given with it प्रथमा विभक्ति एकवचन ending. For example, नरः .

If this were given without an ending, it would appear as नर.

This method is used in many dictionaries and grammar books, and will be explained more fully later.

4. Translating Nouns and Verbs

When a Verb is used with a Noun in the प्रथमा विभक्ति, the words 'he, she, it or they' are not used to translate the Verb ending.
For example:

वृक्षः पतति। means 'The tree falls', NOT 'The tree he falls'

नरः चरति। means 'The man walks', NOT 'The man he walks'

IV. ॥खगः यः वृक्षे तिष्ठति॥

1. एकदा खगः वृक्षे तिष्ठति।

2. फलम् खादति।

3. वने तु नरः चरति।

4. नरः क्षुधितः।

5. सहसा खगम् पश्यति।

6. खगम् खादिष्यामि इति नरः चिन्तयति।

7. फलम् तु पश्यति।

8. खगम् न खादिष्यामि। फलम् खादिष्यामि इति चिन्तयति।

9. हे खग। मह्यम् गाय।

10. साधु गायसि इति नरः वदति।

11. तानि वचनानि श्रुत्वा खगः सन्तुष्टः भवति।

12. सुखेन गायति।

13. तस्मात् फलम् भूमिम् पतति।

14. नरः फलम् हरति।

15. फलम् खादति।

यः — which

1.	एकदा	one day
	वृक्षे	in a tree
2.	फलम्	fruit *(Subject & Object)*
3.	वने	in the forest
	तु	but *(translate first in the sentence)*
4.	क्षुधितः	(is) hungry
5.	सहसा	suddenly
6.	खगम्	bird *(Object)*
	खादिष्यामि	I will eat
	इति	*(see page 15)*
	चिन्तयति	he thinks
8.	न	not
9.	हे	O!
	मह्यम्	to me
	गाय	sing!
10.	साधु गायसि	you sing well
11.	तानि वचनानि	those words
	श्रुत्वा	having heard
	सन्तुष्टः	delighted
12.	गायति	he sings
	सुखेन	happily
13.	तस्मात्	therefore
	भूमिम्	to the ground

Chapter 2 Exercises

Section A

Write down the Subject of each of the following sentences:

(i) Rāma sits in the forest.

(ii) Sītā recites the Gītā.

(iii) Rāma fought against Rāvaṇa.

(iv) Having seen Rāvaṇa, the warriors fled.

(v) I will speak to you.

Section B

(i) *State the* वचन *of the following*

(ii) *Translate each.*

1. रामौ
2. नरौ
3. गजाः
4. रामः
5. गजौ
6. खगाः
7. सिंहौ
8. खगः
9. खगौ
10. नरः

Section C

Translate the following into Sanskrit:

1. We hit
2. They fall
3. Two elephants
4. You eat
5. The trees
6. The two elephants
7. Two lions
8. Men
9. The elephants
10. We eat
11. Rāma
12. We two see
13. Lion
14. The men
15. We two eat
16. You two speak
17. We fall
18. He eats
19. They walk
20. You two see

Section D

(i) *State* *(a) the* वचन (Number)

(b) the पुरुष (Person) *of the following,*

(ii) *Translate each.*

1. वदसि
2. तुदति
3. पततः
4. वदथः
5. तुदामि
6. चरावः
7. पश्यथः
8. वदन्ति
9. पश्यामि
10. खादन्ति

Section E

Translate the following:

1. वदामि।
2. रामः चरति।
3. नराः पश्यन्ति।
4. गजौ चरतः।
5. सिंहाः खादन्ति।
6. रावणः पश्यति।
7. गजाः खादन्ति।
8. नरौ वदतः।
9. गजः चरति।
10. वृक्षाः पतन्ति।

Section F

Translate the following into Sanskrit:

(i) The two trees fall.
(ii) The two men speak.
(iii) The lion eats.
(iv) The two elephants walk.
(v) You two see.
(vi) The birds speak.
(vii) The two lions eat.
(viii) The elephants fall.
(ix) The two men see.
(x) The birds fall.

3. THE MAN AND THE DOG

I. *Vocabulary*:

Learn the following words, and revise those from chapters 1 & 2:

कुक्कुरः	dog
इच्छति	he wants
चिन्तयति	he thinks
धावति	he runs
नयति	he leads
च	and

II. *Grammar:*

Learn the संबोधन of राम, with its meanings.

एकवचन	द्विवचन	बहुवचन	
रामः	रामौ	रामाः	प्रथमा विभक्ति
Rāma	two Rāmas	Rāmas	Nominative
हे राम	हे रामौ	हे रामाः	संबोधन
O Rāma	O two Rāmas	O Rāmas	Vocative

The संबोधन is not a separate विभक्ति. It is merely the प्रथमा used for attracting attention.
Note that the only difference in the forms of Rāma is that the एकवचन does not have a विसर्ग.

III. <u>*Syntax*</u>:

1.The संबोधन

The संबोधन, called the Vocative in English, is used when one is addressing someone. (Vocative comes from the Latin *vocare*, to call.)

<u>The संबोधन Rule</u>
The संबोधन shows who is being called.

For example,

हे रामाः O Rāmas

हे नर वृक्षः पतति। <u>O man</u>, the tree falls.

Note that हे does not have to be used.

For example,

नर कुक्कुरः धावति। <u>O man</u>, the dog runs.

2. And - च

The word च means "and". It is always placed at the end of the group.

For example:

नरः कुक्कुरः च। The man and the dog.

नरः चिन्तयति वदति च। The man thinks and speaks.

3. Two Meanings for the Present Tense

Notice that in English we have two ways of expressing an action which is taking place now: 'he is talking' or 'he talks'. In Sanskrit, the Present form, वदति, may mean either.

IV. ॥नरः कुक्कुरः च॥

1. एकदा नरः पिष्टकम् खादति।

2. नरः प्राज्ञः।

3. कुक्कुरः तम् पश्यति।

4. कुक्कुरः पिष्टकम् पश्यति।

5. कुक्कुरः क्षुधितः।

6. पिष्टकम् इच्छामि इति चिन्तयति।

7. तस्मात् नरम् प्रति धावति।

8. पिष्टकम् हरति।

9. नरात् शीघ्रम् धावति।

10. नरः वदति हे कुक्कुर अपि नवनीतम् इच्छसि इति।

11. पुनः वदति। हे कुक्कुर इच्छसि नवनीतम् इति।

12. कुक्कुरः न किंचित् वदति।

13. तस्मात् नरः वदति हा हा। कुतः कृष्णः न किंचित् माम् वदति इति।

14. सहसा कुक्कुरः कृष्णः भवति।

15.कृष्णः वदति साधु। माम् पश्यसि। अहम् अत्र तत्र सर्वत्र इति।

॥इति कथा॥

Notes on Story 3

1.	एकदा	one day
	पिष्टकम्	bread
2.	प्राज्ञः	is wise
3.	तम्	him
5.	क्षुधितः	is hungry
7.	तस्मात्	therefore
	नरम् प्रति	towards the man
9.	नरात्	away from the man
	शीघ्रम्	quickly
10.	अपि	*makes the sentence a question*
	नवनीतम्	butter
11.	पुनः	again
12.	न किंचित्	nothing
13.	हा हा	Alas! Alas!
	कुतः	why?
	माम्	to me

14.	सहसा	suddenly
15.	साधु	Well done!
	माम्	Me
	अहम्	I am
	अत्र तत्र सर्वत्र	here, there and everywhere

Chapter 3 Exercises

Section A

Copy out the नाम *from the following sentences, and say which ending each should have.*

(i) Rāma walks, O Sītā.
(ii) The dog is standing, O man.
(iii) Where are the dogs, O Lord?
(iv) The warriors fled, O king.
(v) O king, what is Rāma doing?

Section B

(i) *State (a) the* वचन, *and*

(b) the विभक्ति *of each*

(ii) *Translate each.*

1. हे कृष्ण
2. नराः
3. हे गजाः
4. हे राम
5. गजाः
6. खग
7. हे सिंहौ
8. कुक्कुरौ
9. खगाः
10. हे नर

Section C

(i) *State (a) the* वचन *(b) the* पुरुष *of each of the following*

(ii) *Translate each.*

1. इच्छन्ति
2. तुदसि
3. चिन्तयथः
4. वदन्ति
5. पतसि
6. चरामः
7. हरसि
8. धावतः
9. इच्छामि
10. खादथः

Section D

Translate the following into Sanskrit:

1. They want
2. We run
3. You two see
4. They are running
5. The trees fall
6. The dogs
7. You two grab
8. O man
9. I am running
10. O men
11. You think
12. They two grab
13. We two think
14. You see (many)
15. O two Rāmas
16. They speak
17. Two dogs
18. O elephants
19. They think
20. O dogs
21. We two see
22. They are thinking
23. You run
24. O elephant
25. The man is running
26. The two men
27. You two walk
28. They are walking
29. O lions
30. You see, O Kṛṣṇa

Section E

Translate the following:

1. वदसि हे राम।
2. कुक्कुरः चरति।
3. हे नराः पश्यथ।
4. कुक्कुराः चिन्तयन्ति।
5. सिंहाः धावन्ति।
6. गजाः चरन्ति हे कुक्कुर।
7. नराः खादन्ति।
8. नरौ इच्छतः।
9. कृष्णः चिन्तयति।
10. हे राम रावणः चरति।

Section F

Translate the following into English:

1. वदति खादति च।
2. कुक्कुरः नरः च।
3. हे नर कुक्कुर च
4. कुक्कुराः वृक्षाः च।
5. सिंहौ गजः च।
6. चरन्ति धावन्ति च।
7. नराः खादन्ति पश्यन्ति च।
8. कुक्कुरः गजः च।
9. चिन्तयसि चरसि च।
10. नयति खादति च।

Section G

1. Insert the word 'च' into the following, where appropriate:

2. Then translate.

1. खादति चरति
2. सिंहः नरः
3. कुक्कुराः गजाः
4. नयति धावति
5. चिन्तयति पश्यति
6. नरः धावति।
7. हे रामौ कुक्कुरौ
8. खगाः नराः
9. चरन्ति हे राम
10. वृक्षाः गजाः

Section H

Translate the following into Sanskrit:

(i) The men speak, O Rāma.
(ii) They are running, O bird.
(iii) The lions and elephants are eating, O birds.
(iv) The men are walking, O dog.
(v) You two see and run.
(vi) The dogs are running, O man.
(vii) We want and grab.
(viii) They think and run, O Rāma.
(ix) You two see and think.
(x) The two birds fall and walk.

4. THE MAN AND THE ELEPHANT

I. *Vocabulary*:

Learn the following words, and revise those from chapters 1-3.

बालकः	boy
मृगः	deer
पृच्छति	he asks
शृणोति	he hears
भवति	he becomes
गच्छति	he goes

II. *Grammar*:

Learn the द्वितीया विभक्ति of राम, with its meanings.

एकवचन	द्विवचन	बहुवचन	
रामः	रामौ	रामाः	प्रथमा विभक्ति
Rāma	two Rāmas	Rāmas	Nominative
हे राम	हे रामौ	हे रामाः	संबोधन
O Rāma	O two Rāmas	O Rāmas	First Vocative
रामम्	रामौ	रामान्	द्वितीया विभक्ति
Rāma	two Rāmas	Rāmas	Accusative

III. <u>*Syntax*</u>:

1. The द्वितीया विभक्ति rule

(i) The द्वितीया विभक्ति is called the Accusative in English.

(Accusative comes from the Latin *accuso*, 'to accuse' or 'point to')

Learn the following rule by heart.

<u>The द्वितीया विभक्ति Rule</u>
The द्वितीया विभक्ति shows the Object of an action.

For example,

<u>रामम्</u> पश्यति। He sees Rāma.

सिंहः <u>मृगम्</u> खादति। The lion eats <u>the deer</u>.

(ii) The द्वितीया विभक्ति also shows a place to which someone is going

For example,

गजः <u>रामम्</u> चरति। The elephant moves towards Rāma.

2. Word order

In Sanskrit the क्रिया usually comes at the end of the sentence.

For example,

NOT गजः चरति रामम् । The elephant walks to Rāma.

BUT गजः रामम् चरति। The elephant walks to Rāma.

IV. ।।नरः गजः च।।

1. एकदा नरः प्राज्ञम् नरम् गच्छति।
2. नरः प्राज्ञम् नरम् पृच्छति किम् सत्यम् इति।
3. प्राज्ञः नरः वदति सर्वम् ह्येतद् ब्रह्म। अत्र तत्र सर्वत्र आत्मा इति।
4. तानि वचनानि नरः शृणोति सुखी च भवति।
5. गृहम् चरति।
6. मार्गे तु गजम् पश्यति।
7. गजे बालकः उपविशति।
8. बालकः नरम् वदति हे नर किम् करोषि।
9. कुतः गजम् प्रति चरसि इति।
10. नरः चिन्तयति प्राज्ञः नरः वदति अत्र तत्र सर्वत्र आत्मा इति। कुतः अहम् गजात् भीतः इति।
11. नरः पुनः चिन्तयति प्राज्ञः नरः वदति अत्र तत्र सर्वत्र आत्मा इति।
12. नरः गजम् प्रति चरति।

13.सहसा गजः नरम् उद्धरति।

14.नरम् मर्गात् क्षिपति।

15.नरः दुःखी भवति।

16.तस्मात् प्राज्ञम् नरम् पुनः गच्छति।

17.वदति गजः माम् हरति क्षिपति च। आत्मा तु गजे। कुतः आत्मा माम् उद्धरति क्षिपति च इति।

18.प्राज्ञः नरः वदति आत्मा अत्र तत्र सर्वत्र। आत्मा बालके इति॥

Notes on Story 4

1.	एकदा	one day
	प्राज्ञम्	wise
2.	किम्	what is?
	सत्यम्	Truth
	इति	*used instead of speech marks*
3.	प्राज्ञः	wise
	सर्वम् ह्येतद् ब्रह्म	All this is Brahman
	अत्र तत्र सर्वत्र	Here, there and everywhere
	आत्मा	the Self
4.	तानि	those
	वचनानि	words
	सुखी	happy
5.	गृहम्	to his house
6.	मार्गे	on the road
	तु	but *(translate first in the sentence)*
7.	गजे	on the elephant
	उपविशति	is sitting
8.	किम्	what?
	करोषि	are you doing
9.	कुतः	why?
	प्रति	towards *(with the* द्वितीया)
10.	अहम्	I (am)

	गजात्	an elephant
	भीतः	afraid of
11.	पुनः	again
13.	सहसा	suddenly
	उद्धरति	lifts up
14.	मर्गात्	off/away from the road
	क्षिपति	throws
15.	दुःखी	unhappy
16.	तस्मात्	therefore; then
17.	माम्	me
18.	बालके	in the boy

Chapter 4 Exercises

Section A

Copy out the नाम *from the following sentences, and say*

(a) which is the Subject, who is called, and which is the Object.
(b) which विभक्ति *ending each should have.*

1. Rāma sees the man, O Kṛṣṇa.
2. The man walks to the city, O lady.
3. The boys hit Rāma.
4. The men see the boys.
5. The elephants and lions walk, O king.

Section B

For each sentence given below:

1. *Copy out the* नाम.
2. *Say which* विभक्ति *ending each should have.*
3. *Translate the sentence into Sanskrit.*

(i) Rāma sees the elephant, O man.
(ii) The dogs are walking to the elephant.
(iii) The boys walk to Rāma.
(iv) The men are running to Rāma, O boy.
(v) The elephant and the dog run to the boy, O Rāma.

Section C

(i) *State (a) the* वचन *and*

(b) the विभक्ति *of the following*

(ii) *Translate each.*

1. रामान्
2. गजम्
3. हे बालक
4. गजाः
5. हे गज
6. हे नर
7. सिंहौ
8. कुक्कुरम्
9. खगान्
10. बालकौ

Section D

Translate the following into Sanskrit:

1. Two boys (Object)
2. They two run
3. We see
4. You two speak
5. They two go
6. They are going
7. We are running
8. They become
9. The men are asking
10. They speak
11. She becomes
12. They two run
13. We two ask
14. You two become
15. They are becoming
16. The men run
17. We see a boy
18. We two see two boys
19. We run to the boy
20. They run to the lion
21. They see the lions
22. They speak to the man
23. We see the boy
24. You speak to the men
25. You are running
26. They are speaking
27. He goes to the man
28. They are walking to the men
29. We see the boys
30. They are running to the boy

Section E

(i) *State (a) the* वचन *(b) the* पुरुष *of the following*

(ii) *Translate each.*

1. इच्छतः
2. बालकः भवति
3. गच्छन्ति
4. पृच्छामि
5. पतन्ति
6. गच्छामः
7. नयति
8. धावावः
9. भवन्ति
10. खादामः

Section F

Translate the following into English:

1. नराः इच्छन्ति
2. नराः गजान् पश्यन्ति
3. कुक्कुरम् सिंहः पश्यति
4. कुक्कुरः सिंहम् पश्यति
5. वृक्षः पतति
6. चरथ हे नराः
7. नरम् धावामः
8. खगम् खादामि
9. खगाः गजान् पश्यन्ति
10. नराः धावन्ति

Section G

Translate into Sanskrit:

1. The men grab the birds, O Rāma
2. The lions are eating the men.
3. The boy runs to the man.
4. The elephants walk to the trees.
5. The dogs see the lions, O men.

6. The boy speaks and hears.
7. You are running, O lion.
8. They are thinking.
9. The lions see the bird and the dog.
10. They strike the tree, O man.

Section H

Translate the following into English:

1. गजाः सिंहाः च चरन्ति।
2. सिंहः गजम् कुक्कुरम् च पश्यति।
3. नरम् बालकः पृच्छति।
4. नरः बालकम् पृच्छति।
5. हे कुक्कुर नराः चरन्ति।
6. गजान् सिंहान् च पश्यन्ति।
7. नराः धावन्ति चरन्ति च।
8. कुक्कुरम् सिंहः शृणोति।
9. सिंहम् कुक्कुरः शृणोति पश्यति च।
10. हे नर चरसि धावसि च।

Section I

Translate the following into Sanskrit:

One day a man sees a tree. "I want the tree," he thinks. Therefore he walks to the tree. Then he strikes the tree. A boy sees the man and the tree, and says, "Do not hit it". The man becomes frightened and runs. A lion sees the man and runs to the man. He grabs the man and eats him.

One day	एकदा

Do not forget इति at the end of the thought.

therefore/then	तस्मात्
Do not strike it	मा तम् तुद इति
frightened	भीतः
him	तम्

5. THE LION AND THE SHEEP

I. *Vocabulary:*

त्यजति	leaves; abandons	जनकः	father
हस्तः	hand	नादः	roar
खड्गः	sword	मेषः	sheep
रथः	chariot		

II. *Grammar:*

Learn the तृतीया विभक्ति of राम, with its meanings.

एकवचन	द्विवचन	बहुवचन	
रामः	रामौ	रामाः	प्रथमा विभक्ति
Rāma	two Rāmas	Rāmas	Nominative
हे राम	हे रामौ	हे रामाः	संबोधन
O Rāma	O two Rāmas	O Rāmas	Vocative
रामम्	रामौ	रामान्	द्वितीया विभक्ति
Rāma	two Rāmas	Rāmas	Accusative
रामेण	रामाभ्याम्	रामैः	तृतीया विभक्ति
by Rāma	by two Rāmas	by Rāmas	Instrumental

III. <u>*Syntax*</u>:

The तृतीया विभक्ति Rule

Whatever is used for an action is called the instrument. The तृतीया विभक्ति, is called the Instrumental in English, because it is used to show the instrument.

Learn the following rule by heart.

<u>The तृतीया विभक्ति Rule</u>
The तृतीया विभक्ति shows by or with what an action is done.

For example,

<u>रथेन</u> गच्छति। He goes <u>by chariot</u>.

रामः हस्तेन <u>खगम्</u> तुदति। Rāma hits the bird <u>with his hand</u>

Notice that in English we use 'by' or 'with' for the instrument.

IV. ॥सिंहः मेषः च॥

1. एकदा सिंहशावकः वनम् गच्छति।
2. अन्यस्मिन् वने जनकम् अत्यजत्।
3. मेषान् पश्यति।
4. खगान् पश्यति।
5. तस्मात् चिन्तयति कुत्र मम जनकः।
6. मेषान् पश्यामि।
7. मम जनकः अन्यस्मिन् वने वसति।
8. तस्मात् अत्र मेषैः सह वत्स्यामि इति।
9. सिंहशावकः मेषैः सह जीवति।
10. मेषः इव सर्वम् करोति।
11. सहसा तु अन्यः सिंहः वनम् गच्छति।
12. सिंहशावकम् पश्यति।
13. तम् पृच्छति किम् करोषि। मेषः न असि।
14. सिंहः असि इति।
15. सिंहशावकः चिन्तयति अहम् सिंहः अस्मि न मेषः इति।
16. नादम् करोति।
17. मेषाः भीताः वनात् धावन्ति॥

1.	एकदा	one day
	सिंहशावकः	young lion; lion cub
	वनम्	to a forest
2.	अन्यस्मिन् वने	in another forest
	अत्यजत्	he has left, abandoned
5.	तस्मात्	then; therefore
	कुत्र	where is?
	मम	my
7.	वसति	dwell
8.	वत्स्यामि	I will dwell
	अत्र	here
9.	सह	together with *(with the Instrumental)*
	जीवति	lives
10.	इव	like
	सर्वम्	everything
	करोति	he does
11.	सहसा	suddenly
	तु	but
	अन्यः	another
13.	तम्	him
	किम् करोषि	What are you doing?
	न	not
	असि	you are
15.	अहम् अस्मि	I am

16.	करोति	he makes
17.	वनात्	away from/out of the forest
	भीताः	frightened

Chapter 5: Exercises

Section A

Copy out the नाम *from the following sentences, and say*

(a) which is the Subject, who is called, which is the Object and what is used

(b) State which विभक्ति *ending each should have.*

1. Rāma hits the man with a stick, O Kṛṇṣa.
2. The man runs to the town.
3. The dogs are frightened by the sound.
4. The lions eat with their jaws.
5. The men flee away to the city by car.

Section B

Copy out the नाम *from the following sentences, and say which* विभक्ति *ending they should have; then, translate the sentences into Sanskrit.*

(i) The man hits Rāma with a sword.
(ii) O Kṛṣṇa, Rāma goes by chariot to the trees.
(iii) The men see the boys.
(iv) He runs to the tree.
(v) With (his) hand he grabs the boy.

Section C

(i) *State (a) the* वचन *of the following, and*

(b) the विभक्ति

(ii) *Translate each.*

1. रामेण
2. गजान्
3. कुक्कुरम्
4. बालकः
5. जनकेन
6. कृष्णम्
7. नरौ
8. हे गज
9. सिंहौ
10. हस्ताभ्याम्

Section D

Translate the following into Sanskrit:

1. With a hand
2. Boys (Obj.)
3. We are going
4. With two swords
5. O man
6. You two abandon
7. He becomes
8. By means of a sword
9. O men
10. You two want
11. With a dog
12. I hear
13. By a chariot
14. They fall
15. You two see
16. Boys (Subj.)
17. They two walk
18. The dogs
19. The men walk
20. They live
21. They two see
22. With a man
23. I am speaking
24. The boys ask
25. With two hands
26. By chariots
27. We two become
28. He hits the man
29. By hands
30. You two are running

Section E

(i) *State (a) the* वचन

(b) the पुरुष *of the following*

(ii) *Translate each.*

1. त्यजन्ति
2. वसामि
3. जनकेन
4. रामैः
5. सिंहैः
6. धावसि
7. चरतः
8. नराभ्याम्
9. रथान्
10. कुक्कुरेण

Section F

Translate the following into English:

1. खगः रामम् पश्यति।
2. नरः बालकम् हस्तेन नयति।
3. हे नर गजः कुक्कुरम् पश्यति।
4. रामः नरम् रथेन गच्छति।
5. जनकः बालकान् धावति।
6. बालकः गजम् खड्गेन तुदति।
7. नरः खगम् हस्ताभ्याम् खादति।
8. खगाः गजाः च रथम् पश्यन्ति।
9. जनकः कुक्कुरम् त्यजति।
10. नरः कुक्कुरम् हस्तेन तुदति।

Section G

Translate into Sanskrit:

1. The elephant grabs the dog, O man.
2. The men are eating the birds with (their) hands.
3. The dog runs to the tree.
4. The father goes to the tree by chariot.
5. The boy sees the father, O Rāma.
6. The lion sees the dog.
7. The men go by chariots.
8. The boys ask (their) father.
9. The man grabs the boys with (his) hands.
10. They strike the tree with a sword, O man.

Section H

Translate the following into Sanskrit:

One day Rāṃa walks to the forest. He sees a man. The man goes to Rāma, and hits him with a stick. Rāma grabs his sword and walks to the man. He strikes the man with his sword, and the man becomes dead. Rāma says, "You hit me with a stick. Therefore you become dead."

One day	एकदा	therefore	तस्मात्
stick	लगुडः	dead	मृतः
me	माम्		

6. THE MAN AND THE SNAKE

I. *Vocabulary:* Learn the following words.

सर्पः	snake	एकदा	one day
मूषिकः	mouse	सहसा	suddenly
ददाति	he gives	वन्दनम्	thanks
दर्शयति	he shows		

II. *Grammar:*

Learn the चतुर्थी विभक्ति of राम, with its meanings.

एकवचन	द्विवचन	बहुवचन	
रामः	रामौ	रामाः	प्रथमा विभक्ति
Rāma	two Rāmas	Rāmas	Nominative
हे राम	हे रामौ	हे रामाः	संबोधन
O Rāma	O two Rāmas	O Rāmas	Vocative
रामम्	रामौ	रामान्	द्वितीया विभक्ति
Rāma	two Rāmas	Rāmas	Accusative
रामेण	रामाभ्याम्	रामैः	तृतीया विभक्ति
by Rāma	by two Rāmas	by Rāmas	Instrumental
रामाय	रामाभ्याम्	रामेभ्यः	चतुर्थी विभक्ति
for Rāma	for two Rāmas	for Rāmas	Dative

III. Syntax:

The चतुर्थी विभक्ति Rule

The चतुर्थी विभक्ति is called the Dative in English, because it shows the person who receives something. (Dative comes from the Latin *dare*, to give)

Learn the following rule by heart.

The चतुर्थी विभक्ति Rule
The चतुर्थी विभक्ति shows to whom something is offered.

For example,

रथम् रामाय ददाति। He gives a chariot to Rāma.

जनकः कुक्कुरम् बालकाय ददाति। The father gives a dog to the boy.

Notice that:

(i) in English we often miss out the 'to'. For example:
'He gives Rāma a chariot.' = 'He gives a chariot to Rāma.'

(ii) in English we use 'to' for going as well as giving.
For example: He goes to the boy. ('to' after *going*)
He gives the book to the boy. ('to' after *giving*)

The द्वितीया विभक्ति is used for the 'to' after *going*:

He goes to the boy. = बालकम् गच्छति।

He walks to Rāma. = रामम् चरति।

The चतुर्थी विभक्ति is used for the 'to' after *giving*:

He gives the snake to the boy. = सर्पम् बालकाय ददाति।

The thing which is given is the Object of the action of giving, and therefore takes the द्वितीया विभक्ति ending.

IV. ॥ नरः सर्पः च ॥

1. एकदा नरः नगरम् चरति।

2. मार्गे सर्पम् पश्यति।

3. सर्पः विशालः घोरः च।

4. नरः तु प्राज्ञः अभयः च।

5. नरः चिन्तयति अत्र सर्पः घोरः। किम् करिष्यामि। मम गुरुः नित्यम् वदति अत्र तत्र सर्वत्र आत्मा। तस्मात् आत्मा सर्पे। तम् वदिष्यामि इति।

6. तस्मात् वदति हे कृष्ण। तव रूपात् अहम् भीतः। दर्शय मह्यम् तव प्रियम् रूपम् इति।

7. सहसा तु घोरः विशालः च सर्पः अल्पः मूषिकः भवति।

8. नरः सन्तुष्टः भवति।

9. हे कृष्ण। वन्दनम् इति वदति।

10. नगरम् च चरति।

Notes

1.	नगरम्	to a town
2.	मार्गे	on the road
3.	विशालः घोरः च	large and horrible
4.	तु	but *(translate first in the sentence)*
	प्राज्ञः	wise
	अभयः	fearless
5.	अत्र	here is
	किम् करिष्यामि	what will I do?
	मम गुरुः	my teacher
	नित्यम्	always
	अत्र तत्र सर्वत्र	here, there and everywhere
	आत्मा	the Self
	सर्पे	in the snake
	तस्मात्	therefore
	तम्	to him
	वदिष्यामि	I will speak
6.	तव	your
	रूपात्	form
	भीतः	I am frightened of
	दर्शय मह्यम्	show me!
	प्रियम्	pleasant
	रूपम्	form

7. अल्पः	small
8. सन्तुष्टः	contented
9. वन्दनम्	thanks

Chapter 6: Exercises

Section A

Copy out the नाम *from the following sentences, and say which* विभक्ति *ending each should have.*

1. Rāma gives the book to a friend.
2. O man, the lady walks to the town.
3. The elephant hits the dog with (his) trunk.
4. The kings give food to the men.
5. Are the men eating the food with (their) hands and giving drinks to the ladies?

Section B

Copy out the नाम *from the following sentences, and say which* विभक्ति *ending they should have; then, translate the sentences into Sanskrit.*

(i) The snake eats the mouse.
(ii) Rāma gives the dog to Kṛṣṇa.
(iii) The man shows the elephant to the boy.
(iv) The boys show the dogs to the elephants.
(v) Suddenly Rāma hits the boy with (his) hand.

Section C

(i) *State (a) the* वचन *of the following, and (b) the* विभक्ति

(ii) *Translate each.*

1. सर्पाय
2. मूषिकान्
3. कुक्कुराभ्याम्
4. मूषिकेन
5. रथाय
6. गजम्
7. सिंहेभ्यः
8. हे सर्प
9. नरैः
10. बालकैः

Section D

Translate the following into Sanskrit:

1. For the boys
2. O men
3. We show
4. For the snakes
5. We live
6. For the man
7. They become
8. With a chariot
9. You are speaking
10. They two want
11. For two snakes
12. You two see
13. With the lions
14. They speak
15. Suddenly they are walking
16. Trees (Subj.)
17. They two walk
18. The snakes
19. By the mice
20. I show
21. For the boy
22. To the man
23. They are saying
24. The boys show
25. By a mouse
26. He gives
27. For the dogs
28. By the elephants
29. You show
30. He grabs the boys

Section E

(i) *State (a) the* वचन *(b) the* पुरुष *of the following*

(ii) *Translate each.*

1. त्यजमि
2. दर्शयामि
3. पश्यतः
4. गच्छसि
5. चरथ
6. ददासि
7. वदामि
8. भवन्ति
9. खादथः
10. पश्यन्ति

Section F

Translate the following into English:

1. रामः मूषिकम् बालकाय ददाति।
2. नरः सर्पम् रामाय ददाति।
3. रथेन गजम् गच्छति।
4. खगम् बालकेभ्यः ददाति।
5. हे कृष्ण नराः बालकम् पश्यन्ति।
6. सिंहः कुक्कुरम् धावति।
7. सहसा नरम् हस्तेन तुदति।
8. बालकः खगम् नराय ददाति।
9. हस्ताभ्याम् गजम् नराः तुदन्ति।
10. नरः मूषिकान् खगेभ्यः ददाति।

Section G

Translate into Sanskrit:

1. The man gives the tree to the boys, O Rāma.
2. The boys see the lions and the elephants.
3. He shows the snake to the mice.
4. The dogs run to the man and the tree.
5. The boy gives the snake to the men.
6. The men walk to the trees, O Kṛṣṇa.
7. The men grab the snakes.
8. The lions eat the dogs.
9. Suddenly the man grabs the boy with his hand, O Rāma.
10. One day the man gives the boy a bird.

Section H

Translate the following into Sanskrit:

One day a man walks to a tree. He sees a mouse and a snake. He grabs the mouse with his hand. The mouse becomes frightened, and says to the man, "Why do you grab me with (your) hand, o man?" The man says to the mouse, "Snakes eat mice."

frightened	भीतः	why	कुतः

7. THE MAN AND THE TREE

I. *Vocabulary:* Learn the following words.

तिष्ठति	he stands	कथम्	how?
आगच्छति	he comes	न	not
दूतः	messenger		
गोविन्दः	Govinda *(a name of the Absolute)*		

II. *Grammar*

Learn the पञ्चमी विभक्ति of रामः, with its meanings.

एकवचन	द्विवचन	बहुवचन	
रामः	रामौ	रामाः	प्रथमा विभक्ति
Rāma	two Rāmas	Rāmas	Nominative
हे राम	हे रामौ	हे रामाः	संबोधन
O Rāma	O two Rāmas	O Rāmas	Vocative
रामम्	रामौ	रामान्	द्वितीया विभक्ति
Rāma	two Rāmas	Rāmas	Accusative
रामेण	रामाभ्याम्	रामैः	तृतीया विभक्ति
by Rāma	by two Rāmas	by Rāmas	Instrumental
रामाय	रामाभ्याम्	रामेभ्यः	चतुर्थी विभक्ति
for Rāma	for two Rāmas	for Rāmas	Dative
रामात्	रामाभ्याम्	रामेभ्यः	पञ्चमी विभक्ति
from Rāma	from two Rāmas	from Rāmas	Ablative

III. *Syntax*:

1. The पञ्चमी विभक्ति rule

The पञ्चमी विभक्ति is called the Ablative in English, because it shows from where something comes. (Ablative comes from the Latin *ablatum*, carried away from.)

Learn the following rule by heart.

The पञ्चमी विभक्ति Rule
The पञ्चमी विभक्ति shows from where something comes.

For example,

नरः रामात् धावति। The man runs from Rāma.

जनकः कुक्कुरम् बालकात् नयति। The father leads the dog from the boy.

2. The negative – 'not'

The word न is used in Sanskrit to negate a sentence.

For example, धावति means 'he runs'.

न धावति means 'he does not run.'

न is placed immediately before the क्रिया.

For example,

नरः रामात् न धावति। The man does not run from Rāma.

रामः कुक्कुरम् बालकात् न नयति। Rāma does not lead the dog from the boy.

IV. ।।नरः वृक्षः च।।

1. एकदा नरः वने तिष्ठति।

2. विशालम् वृक्षम् पश्यति।

3. वृक्षे बहूनि पर्णानि।

4. नरः चिन्तयति कथम् प्राज्ञः भवामि।

5. न कुत्रचित् गोविन्दम् पश्यामि इति।

6. सहसा तु दूतः गोविन्दात् आगच्छति।

7. दूतः वदति हे नर। गोविन्दः वदति यथा वृक्षे बहूनि पर्णानि सन्ति तथा बहुकालम् गोविन्दम् न द्रक्ष्यसि इति।

8. नरः सुखी भवति।

9. वन्दनम् वन्दनम् हे गोविन्द इति वदति।

10. दूतः चिन्तयति किम् करोति। बहुकालम् गोविन्दम् न द्रक्ष्यति इति।

11. दूतः वदति किम् करोषि। बहुकालम् गोविन्दम् न द्रक्ष्यसि इति।

12.नरः वदति अहम् सुखी। गोविन्दम् द्रक्ष्यामि इति।

13.गोविन्दः नरस्य वचनानि शृणोति नरम् च आगच्छति।

1.	वने	in a forest
2.	विशालम्	large
3.	वृक्षे	on the tree
	बहूनि पर्णानि।	many leaves
4.	प्राज्ञः	wise
5.	कुत्रचित्	anywhere
6.	तु	but *(translate first)*
7.	यथा	just as
	सन्ति	there are
	तथा	so
	बहुकालम्	for a long time
	द्रक्ष्यति	he will see *(takes endings like* भवति*)*
8.	सुखी	happy
10.	किम् करोति	What is he doing?
11.	किम् करोषि	What are you doing?
	अहम्	I (am)
13.	नरस्य	of the man
	वचनानि	words

Chapter 7: Exercises

Section A

Copy out the नाम *from the following sentences, and say which* विभक्ति *ending each should have.*

1.The men go from the town to the house.
2.The bird falls from the tree, O Rāma.
3.The book comes from the shop.
4.The lion comes from the forest by foot.
5.The man gives the lady a book from the town with his hand, Rāma.

Section B

Copy out the नाम *from the following sentences, and say which* विभक्ति *ending they should have; then, translate the sentences into Sanskrit.*

(i) The messenger comes by chariot to the boy.
(ii) O Rāma, the boys are coming from their father.
(iii)The father gives the boy a bird from the tree.
(iv)How does the mouse run from the man, O Govinda?
(v) The snake comes from the boys to the man by chariot.

Section C

(i) *State (a) the* वचन *of the following, and (b) the* विभक्ति

(ii) *Translate each.*

1. गोविन्दात्
2. सिंहाभ्याम्
3. गजेन
4. नराः
5. हस्तेन
6. रामेण
7. मूषिकम्
8. सर्पाय
9. रथैः
10. जनकाः

Section D

Translate the following into Sanskrit:

1. They abandon
2. How does he speak?
3. To a mouse
4. For a messenger
5. They speak
6. We fall
7. From a roar
8. For a father
9. They show
10. The dogs run
11. Govinda comes
12. They stand
13. For a elephant
14. He asks
15. You go
16. He stands
17. From a chariot
18. By a snake
19. By hands
20. You run
21. With a sword
22. From a messenger
23. You give
24. You think
25. Suddenly they speak
26. The man goes
27. From a bird
28. From the boys
29. We lead
30. By a mouse

Section E

(i) *State (a) the* वचन *(b) the* पुरुष *of the following*

(ii) *Translate each.*

1. तिष्ठति
2. ददामि
3. भवन्ति
4. चरामः
5. पश्यामि
6. आगच्छसि
7. शृणोति
8. चिन्तयतः
9. पतति
10. तुदावः

Section F

Translate the following:

1. न भवति
2. न चरसि
3. न पतामः
4. न भवावः
5. न त्यजन्ति
6. न तुदन्ति
7. न चिन्तयसि
8. शृणोति
9. न तिष्ठति
10. न ददासि

Section G

Translate the following into Sanskrit:

1. They do not stand
2. The mouse does not run
3. A snake does not hear
4. We stand
5. They do not speak
6. He does not speak
7. The chariot does not fall
8. The messengers do not come
9. The boys do not walk
10. You do not run

Section H

Translate the following into English:

1. हे राम कथम् नरः गच्छति।
2. मूषिकः नरात् बालकात् च आगच्छति।
3. नरम् हस्तेन न तुदति।
4. सिंहः मूषिकम् बालकाय न ददाति।
5. नराः रथात् पतन्ति।
6. कुक्कुरम् बालकः हस्तेन तुदति।
7. कथम् बालकः मूषिकम् गजम् च न पश्यति।
8. कथम् दूतः नरम् वदति।
9. गोविन्दः रथात् नरम् आगच्छति।
10. रामः सिंहाय बालकम् न ददाति।

Section I

Translate into Sanskrit:

1. The man and the boy see Govinda from the chariot.
2. The mouse does not stand.
3. The dogs run from the snake to the boy.
4. One day the boy sees Rāma.
5. The father strikes the boy from the chariot with his sword.
6. The boy gives his father a bird from the tree.
7. Suddenly he strikes the tree with his sword.
8. We do not walk to the elephant from the chariot.
9. You (many) do not ask the father.
10. The lion does not see the mouse.

8. THE SON AND THE FATHER

I. *Vocabulary:* Learn the following words.

पुत्रः	son	अत्र	here
अश्वः	horse	बहुकालम्	for a long time
जीवति	he lives	तु	but

II. *Grammar:*

Learn the षष्ठी विभक्ति of राम, with its meanings.

एकवचन	द्विवचन	बहुवचन	
रामः	रामौ	रामाः	प्रथमा विभक्ति
Rāma	two Rāmas	Rāmas	Nominative
हे राम	हे रामौ	हे रामाः	संबोधन
O Rāma	O two Rāmas	O Rāmas	Vocative
रामम्	रामौ	रामान्	द्वितीयाविभक्ति
Rāma	two Rāmas	Rāmas	Accusative
रामेण	रामाभ्याम्	रामैः	तृतीया विभक्ति
by Rāma	by two Rāmas	by Rāmas	Instrumental
रामाय	रामाभ्याम्	रामेभ्यः	चतुर्थी विभक्ति
for Rāma	for two Rāmas	for Rāmas	Dative
रामात्	रामाभ्याम्७	रामेभ्यः	पञ्चमी विभक्ति
from Rāma	from two Rāmas	from Rāmas	Ablative
रामस्य	रामयोः	रामाणाम्	षष्ठी विभक्ति
of Rāma	of two Rāmas	of Rāmas	Genitive

III. *Syntax*:

1. The षष्ठी विभक्ति Rule

(i) The षष्ठी विभक्ति is called the Genitive in English. (Genitive comes from the Latin Latin root *gen-*, to produce, which gives English words like generate and generation)

Learn the following rule by heart.

The षष्ठी विभक्ति Rule
The षष्ठी विभक्ति shows who has something.

For example,

रामस्य रथः Rāma's chariot.

जनकस्य कुक्कुरम् पश्यति। He sees the father's dog.

(ii) In Sanskrit the नाम in the षष्ठी comes first. Likewise, in English we say "The man's boat", although we can also say, "The boat of the man."

For example: रामस्य पुत्रः NOT पुत्रः रामस्य.

2. But - तु

The word तु means 'but'. It is always placed after the first word in the sentence, never at the beginning.

For example:

रामस्य तु रथम् पश्यामि। But I see Rāma's chariot.

IV. ॥ पुत्रः जनकः च ॥

1. एकदा पुत्रः जनकात् वनम् अश्वेन गच्छति।

2. वने सिंहान् गजान् च पश्यति।

3. चिन्तयति अत्र अहम् सन्तुष्टः। जनकम् न गमिष्यामि इति।

4. बहुकालम् सन्तुष्टः वने जीवति।

5. सहसा तु सिंहस्य नादम् शृणोति।

6. तस्मात् भीतः भवति।

7. सिंहात् धावति।

8. चिन्तयति जनकम् गमिष्यामि इति।

9. तस्मात् जनकम् धावति।

10. पुत्रः जनकम् पश्यति।

11. जनकः पुत्रम् पश्यति।

12. हे गोविन्द। वन्दनम्। मम पुत्रः आगच्छति। मम पुत्रम् पश्यामि इति जनकः वदति।

13. पुत्रः वदति वन्दनम् हे गोविन्द। मम जनकम् पश्यामि इति।

3.	अहम्	I am
	सन्तुष्टः	happy; contented
4.	वने	in the forest
5.	गमिष्यामि	I will go
6.	तस्मात्	therefore
	भीतः	frightened
12.	वन्दनम्	thank you
	मम	my

Chapter 8: Exercises

Section A

Copy out the नाम *from the following sentences, and say which* विभक्ति *ending each should have.*

1. The dog eats the flesh of the sheep.
2. The man sees John's wife.
3. The elephant strikes the lady with his tail.
4. The king's work does not harm the subjects.
5. The lions are eating the flesh of the dog and giving it to the beasts.

Section B

(a) Copy out the Nouns from the following sentences,
(b) say which विभक्ति *ending they should have,*
(c) translate the sentences into Sanskrit.

(i) For a long time the snake eats the mouse.
(ii) The son's father sees the horse.
(iii) The boy gives the horse of (his) father to the son of the man.
(iv) The man hits Rāma's son with his hand.
(v) The boys run from the elephants to the horses.

Section C

(i) *State (a) the* वचन *of the following, and (b) the* विभक्ति

(ii)*Translate each.*

1. रामयोः	6. हे पुत्र
2. अश्वैः	7. कुक्कुरान्
3. पुत्रस्य	8. गजानाम्
4. बालकात्	9. रामाभ्याम्
5. पुत्रेभ्यः	10. अश्वानाम्

Section D

Translate the following into Sanskrit:

1. They live
2. You see
3. We run
4. By a son
5. With the dogs
6. To the men
7. For the boy
8. Of the man
9. From the dogs
10. Of the boys
11. You (Pl.) live
12. Of the horse
13. They say
14. I think
15. By Rāmas
16. Of a lion
17. With the lions
18. By the horses
19. Of the two sons
20. He says
21. I live
22. He asks
23. They come
24. Of the messenger
25. From the horse
26. Of the sons
27. By the elephant
28. Dogs (Obj.)
29. We fall
30. O Kṛṣṇa

Section E

(i) *State (a) the* वचन *(b) the* पुरुष *of the following*

(ii) *Translate each.*

1. जीवसि	6. पश्यामि
2. गच्छथ	7. चिन्तयसि
3. धावन्ति	8. आगच्छामः
4. तिष्ठतः	9. पतन्ति
5. चरसि	10. तुदावः

Section F

Translate the following into English:

1. रामस्य पुत्रः वृक्षम् गच्छति।
2. अत्र तु पुत्रस्य अश्वाः जीवन्ति।
3. रामः बालकाय अश्वम् ददाति।
4. गजाः सिंहाः च रामात् धावन्ति।
5. अत्र बालकस्य रथः तिष्ठति।
6. पुत्राणाम् अश्वाः रथः च तिष्ठन्ति।
7. गोविन्दस्य खगान् सिंहाः खादन्ति।
8. गोविन्दस्य दूतः रामम् आगच्छति।
9. कथम् अश्वम् नरस्य पुत्राय ददासि।
10. नराणाम् रथाः न आगच्छन्ति।

Section G

Translate into Sanskrit:

1. The father's son lives here.
2. The boys and the men are running to the trees.
3. For a long time the boy's horse runs to the man.
4. The man hits the dogs with his hands.
5. We give the man's trees to the boys.
6. How does Rāma eat the bird with his hand?
7. The boys are walking to the men.
8. The sons of the fathers are running from the man's hand.
9. The birds fall from the trees.
10. Govinda's messenger is not coming from the tree.

9. THE TWO BIRDS

I. *<u>Vocabulary</u>:* Learn the following words.

मार्गः	road; path	चिरेण	after a while
अचलः	mountain	कुतः	why?
नित्यम्	always		

II. *<u>Grammar</u>:* Learn the सप्तमी विभक्ति of राम.

एकवचन	द्विवचन	बहुवचन	
रामः	रामौ	रामाः	प्रथमा विभक्ति
Rāma	two Rāmas	Rāmas	Nominative
हे राम	हे रामौ	हे रामाः	संबोधन
O Rāma	O two Rāmas	O Rāmas	Vocative
रामम्	रामौ	रामान्	द्वितीया विभक्ति
Rāma	two Rāmas	Rāmas	Accusative
रामेण	रामाभ्याम्	रामैः	तृतीया विभक्ति
by Rāma	by two Rāmas	by Rāmas	Instrumental
रामाय	रामाभ्याम्	रामेभ्यः	चतुर्थी विभक्ति
for Rāma	for two Rāmas	for Rāmas	Dative
रामात्	रामाभ्याम्	रामेभ्यः	पञ्चमी विभक्ति
from Rāma	from two Rāmas	from Rāmas	Ablative
रामस्य	रामयोः	रामाणाम्	षष्ठी विभक्ति
of Rāma	of two Rāmas	of Rāmas	Genitive
रामे	रामयोः	रामेषु	सप्तमी विभक्ति
in/on Rāma	in/on two Rāmas	in/on Rāmas	Locative

III. *Syntax*:

The सप्तमी विभक्ति Rule

The सप्तमी विभक्ति is called the Locative in English, because it shows the *place* where something happens. (Locative comes from the Latin *locus*, place.)

Learn the following rule by heart.

The सप्तमी विभक्ति Rule
The सप्तमी विभक्ति shows where an action happens.

For example,

मार्गे नरः तिष्ठति। The man stands on the road.

गजे बालकः वदति। The boy speaks on the elephant.

वृक्षे नरः तिष्ठति। The man stands in the tree.

IV. ॥द्वौ खगौ॥

1. एकदा द्वौ खगौ वृक्षे तिष्ठतः।
2. प्रथमः खगः नित्यम् फलानि खादति।
3. तस्मात् सन्तुष्टः भवति।
4. अन्यः खगः वृक्षे तिष्ठति।
5. फलानि न खादति।
6. सर्वम् तु पश्यति।
7. चिरेण प्रथमः खगः दुःखी भवति।
8. चिन्तयति हा हा किम् करोमि। फलम् नित्यम् न इच्छामि इति।
9. द्वितीयः तु खगः नित्यम् सन्तुष्टः तिष्ठति।
10. द्वितीयः खगः गोविन्दः इव सर्वम् पश्यति।
11. प्रथमः खगः द्वितीयम् खगम् पश्यति।
12. तस्मात् चिन्तयति कुतः अहम् दुःखी। अन्यः तु खगः सुखी इति।
13. तस्मात् अन्यम् खगम् पृच्छति कुतः अहम् दुःखी। त्वम् तु नित्यम् सुखी इति।

14. द्वितीयः खगः वदति प्राज्ञाः नराः सर्वम् पश्यन्ति। न तु किंचित् इच्छन्ति।।

1.	द्वौ	two
2.	प्रथमः	the first
	फलानि	fruits
3.	तस्मात्	therefore
	सन्तुष्टः	contented; happy
4.	अन्यः	the other
6.	सर्वम्	everything
	दुःखी	unhappy
8.	हा हा	alas, alas
	किम् करोमि	What am I doing?
	फलम्	fruit
9.	द्वितीयः	second
10.	इव	like *(see chapter 14)*
12.	अहम्	am I
	सुखी	happy
13.	त्वम्	you (are)
	प्राज्ञाः	wise
14.	न किंचित्	nothing

Chapter 9: Exercises

Section A

Copy out the नाम *from the following sentences, and say which* विभक्ति *ending each should have.*

1. The men stand on the ground.
2. The boys give the book to the man, O lady.
3. They see the boy in the house.
4. The man runs from the house to the forest.
5. The boys' father eats the food with his hand.

Section B

Copy out the नाम *from the following sentences, and say which* विभक्ति *ending they should have; then, translate the sentences into Sanskrit.*

(i) The dog runs from the mountain.
(ii) The men go to the tree by chariot.
(iii) The birds live in the tree.
(iv) The father's son grabs the bird from the tree.
(v) The boy gives (his) father birds.

Section C

(i) *State (a) the* वचन *of the following, and*
(b) the विभक्ति

(ii) *Translate each.*

1.	कुक्कुराभ्याम्	6.	हस्तेन
2.	गोविन्दाय	7.	रथैः
3.	गजात्	8.	जनकानाम्
4.	अश्वौ	9.	हस्तात्
5.	सर्पस्य	10.	अश्वाः

Section D

Translate the following into Sanskrit:

1. They run
2. Away from a horse
3. Of the lion
4. You live
5. You (many) say
6. For a man
7. We see
8. They fall
9. He eats
10. On a elephant
11. Away from the water
12. We two come
13. I leave
14. We two run
15. You many speak
16. By feet
17. In a mountain
18. They leave
19. We two walk
20. From a mouse
21. The man's tree
22. I hit
23. You two go
24. Of Govinda
25. On the path
26. In the mountains
27. You give
28. The horse falls
29. With a roar
30. By a lion

Section E

(i) *State (a) the* वचन

(b) the पुरुष *of the following*

(ii) *Translate each.*

1. तुदति
2. चिन्तयतः
3. हरामः
4. पृच्छति
5. जीवसि
6. खादन्ति
7. धावति
8. भवन्ति
9. गच्छावः
10. तिष्ठथ

Section F

Translate the following into English:

1. नित्यम् गोविन्दः नरान् पश्यति।
2. कुतः गजे नरः तिष्ठति।
3. मार्गे सर्पाः कुक्कुरः च न तिष्ठन्ति।
4. जनकस्य बालकः वृक्षात् पतति।
5. सिंहाः गजाः च मूषिकान् न खादन्ति।
6. गजः बालकः च वृक्षम् चरतः।
7. नरः बालकम् हस्तेन खड्गेन च तुदति।
8. जनकः बालकाय अश्वम् ददाति।
9. बालकः गजम् पृच्छति कथम् चरसि हे गज इति।
10. नित्यम् खगाः मूषिकान् खादन्ति।

Section G

Translate into Sanskrit:

1. The lions always eat the elephants.
2. The boys are standing in the trees.
3. The men give the boys the mice.
4. I ask the boys, "How do you walk to the tree?"
5. The boys do not hit (their) father with (their) hands.
6. The man is standing on the path.
7. The boy's father pushes the mouse with (his) hand.
8. We run from the tree to the mountains.
9. Father, why do we live in the mountains?
10. Govinda's messenger does not speak to men.

Part 2:
Chapters 10-18

SCRIPTURE

श्रीभगवानुवाच।

अशोच्यानन्वशोचस्त्वं प्रज्ञावादांश्च भाषसे।

गतासूनगतासूंश्च नानुशोचन्ति पण्डिताः॥११॥

न त्वेवाहं जातु नासं न त्वं नेमे जनाधिपाः।

न चैव न भविष्यामः सर्वे वयमतः परम्॥१२॥

देहिनोऽस्मिन्यथा देहे कौमारं यौवनं जरा।

तथा देहान्तरप्राप्तिर्धीरस्तत्र न मुह्यति॥१३॥

मात्रास्पर्शास्तु कौन्तेय शीतोष्णसुखदुःखदाः।

आगमापायिनोऽनित्यास्तांस्तितिक्षस्व भारत॥१४॥

यं हि न व्यथयन्त्येते पुरुषं पुरुषर्षभ।

समदुःखसुखं धीरं सोऽमृतत्वाय कल्पते॥१५॥

नासतो विद्यते भावो नाभावो विद्यते सतः।

उभयोरपि दृष्टोऽन्तस्त्वनयोस्तत्त्वदर्शिभिः॥१६॥

अविनाशि तु तद्विद्धि येन सर्वमिदं ततम्।

विनाशमव्ययस्यास्य न कश्चित्कर्तुमर्हति॥१७॥

[The blessed Lord Shrī Kṛṣṇa gently smiled:]

"You speak with some intelligence, yet grieve. 11
What right can sorrow claim? The wise grieve not;
In life and death they find no cause to mourn.
There never was a time when I was not, 12
Nor when these kings, and you, did not exist,
Nor shall there be a time when we have ceased.
A single body passes through each age 13
As men grow old; so does the Spirit pass
Through cycles of these brief embodiments.
Wise men are not disturbed by such events.
O son of Kuntī, bear all things of sense; 14
They are impermanent; they rise and fall.
Bear heat and cold, sweet pleasure and dire pain,
Born from mere contact of objects with their sense.
Be worthy of the kin of Bharata!
That steady man unshaken by these trials, 15
For whom such fleeting moments are the same,
Proves fit indeed for immortality.
What is not real does not in fact exist; 16
That which is real exists eternally:
Who knows this difference sees the final truth.
Time cannot move the substance of all things; 17
Immutable, it cannot be destroyed.

(Bhagavad Gītā, Chapter II, vv.11-17*)*

10. THE ELEPHANT AND THE CROCODILE

I. *Vocabulary:* Learn the following words.

पिबति	drinks	पादः	foot
क्रोशति	cries out	लोकः	world
वसति	dwells	स्वर्गः	heaven
समुद्रः	ocean; sea	भागः	part; portion
मत्स्यः	fish	वर्षः	year
मकरः	crocodile	जलाधारः	lake; pond

II. *Grammar:*

The Three Aspects of Time

1. There are three aspects to Time: Past, Present and Future. In Western Grammar the word 'Tense' is used, so we speak of the Present Tense, Past Tense and Future Tense of a क्रिया or Verb. The Present Tense indicates what is happening at the time when someone is speaking, the Past Tense indicates that which has happened before someone speaks and the Future that which will happen afterwards.

Present Tense	What is happening now
Past Tense	What happened before
Future Tense	What will happen afterwards

2. The Future - भविष्यति

Learn the Future Tense of भवति with its meanings.

भविष्यति he will become	भविष्यतः they two will become	भविष्यन्ति they will become
भविष्यसि you will become	भविष्यथः you two will become	भविष्यथ you will become
भविष्यामि I shall become	भविष्यावः we two shall become	भविष्यामः we shall become

The endings are exactly the same as those for the Present Tense, but the Stem to which they are added has been changed. In most cases an इष्य is added in between the Stem and the ending. This does not happen in all cases (see below).

3. Learn the following table of the Future forms of some of the क्रिया which you know. Note that some of them may be a little different from what you expected!

Present	Meaning	Future	Meaning
वदति	says	वदिष्यति	will say
पतति	falls	पतिष्यति	will fall
चरति	walks	चरिष्यति	will walk
तुदति	hits	तोत्स्यति	will hit
चिन्तयति	thinks	चिन्तयिष्यति	will think
धावति	runs	धाविष्यति	will run
भवति	becomes	भविष्यति	will become
गच्छति	goes	गमिष्यति	will go
आगच्छति	comes	आगमिष्यति	will come
जीवति	lives	जीविष्यति	will live
ददाति	gives	दास्यति	will give
शृणोति	hears	श्रोष्यति	will hear
पश्यति	sees	द्रक्ष्यति	will see

IV. ॥मकरः गजः च॥

1. एकदा गजः वने चरति।

2. सहसा जलाधारम् पश्यति।

3. जलाधारम् गच्छति।

4. जलम् पिबति।

5. जलाधारे विशालः घोरः च मकरः वसति।

6. मकरः गजम् पश्यति।

7. चिन्तयति गजम् खादिष्यामि इति।

8. गजस्य पादम् हरति।

9. गजः क्रोशति हा हा। हे गोविन्द। किम् करिष्यामि इति।

10. जले पुष्पम् पश्यति।

11. पुष्पम् गोविन्दाय ददाति।

12. वदति हे गोविन्द माम् रक्ष इति।

13. गोविन्दः स्वर्गात् आगच्छति।

14. मकरम् हस्तेन तुदति।

15. गजः मुक्तः भवति।

16.चिरेण गजः मकरम् स्वर्गे पश्यति।

17.गोविन्दम् पृच्छति हे गोविन्द। कुतः मकरः स्वर्गे तिष्ठति इति।

18.गोविन्दः तु वदति साधुः मकरः। तस्मात् स्वर्गे वसति। त्वम् न हतः।

19.इदानीम् लोके वससि इति।

1.	वने	in a forest
4.	जलम्	water
5.	विशालः	large
	घोरः	horrible
9.	किम् करिष्यामि	What will I do?
10.	जले	on the water
	पुष्पम्	a flower
12.	माम् रक्ष	Save me!
15.	मुक्तः	free
18.	साधुः	good; virtuous
	तस्मात्	therefore
	त्वम्	you (are)
	हतः	killed *(you have not been)*
19.	इदानीम्	now

Chapter 10: Exercises

Section A

For each sentence, state:

(a) the नाम *and say which* विभक्ति *ending each should have.*

(b) the क्रिया *and its Tense.*

1. The men will run from the town to the house.
2. They see the dogs from the mountain.
3. We will go to the mountains, O Kṛṣṇa.
4. I will speak to the son of the king.
5. They give the present to the boys.

Section B

Copy out the नाम *from the following sentences, and say which* विभक्ति *ending they will take; then, translate the sentences into Sanskrit.*

(i) We will run to the snake.
(ii)They are giving the bird to the snake.
(iii)You will see the man.
(iv)The snake will go from the tree to the lion.
(v)The boys are running from the man.

Section C

(i) *State the Tense of each of the following,*
(ii) *then translate.*

1. धाविष्यन्ति
2. भवसि
3. गमिष्यामि
4. पृच्छामः
5. वदिष्यतः
6. खादिष्यसि
7. चरामः
8. द्रक्ष्यथ
9. इच्छतः
10. चरिष्यावः

Section D

(i) *State (a) the* वचन *of the following, and*

(b) the विभक्ति

(ii) *Translate each.*

1. रामस्य
2. हस्तेन
3. अचले
4. मूषिकानाम्
5. रथेभ्यः
6. गजात्
7. बालकान्
8. सर्पयोः
9. कुक्कुराय
10. हे खग

Section E

Translate the following into Sanskrit:

1. You abandon
2. You will eat
3. They two will fall
4. From a fish
5. I grab
6. Of Govinda
7. They will hit
8. We live
9. You two will not speak
10. He shows
11. By a sword
12. In the mountains
13. We will walk
14. Of the boys
15. I will come
16. They dwell
17. From the elephants
18. Of a father
19. With hands
20. You give
21. I hear
22. By horse
23. They will not run
24. From the sea
25. They do not stand
26. From the trees
27. In the world
28. They will think
29. He drinks
30. We cry out

Section F

(i) *State (a) the* वचन *(b) the* पुरुष *and (c) Tense of the following,*

(ii) *Translate each.*

1. भविष्यामि
2. आगमिष्यतः
3. वदिष्यावः
4. त्यजतः
5. द्रक्ष्यसि
6. तुदति
7. खादिष्यति
8. गच्छामः
9. धावन्ति
10. चिन्तयथ

Section G

Translate the following into English

1. सहसा नरः अचलात् वृक्षम् धावति।
2. रामस्य दूतः सिंहम् गमिष्यति।
3. नराय गजम् ददामि।
4. बालकाः जनकाः च अश्वैः अचलान् न आगमिष्यन्ति।
5. मूषिकः अचलम् त्यजति।
6. बालकः नरम् पृच्छति कुतः पिबसि इति।
7. नरः पादेन हस्तेन च गजान् तुदति।
8. सर्पः गजम् सिंहम् च न तोत्स्यति।
9. नरम् वदिष्यामि कथम् अचलेषु वससि इति।
10. चिरेण बालकाः मत्स्यान् खादिष्यन्ति।

Section H

Translate into Sanskrit:

1. The boys are dwelling in the mountains.
2. The men will run to the tree and hit the lion.
3. Govinda will say to the men, "O men, how will you go?"
4. Suddenly the men run from the mountains to the trees.
5. Govinda gives men chariots and horses.
6. The men will hit the boys with (their) hands.
7. They are going to the mountains.
8. The snakes are living in the trees.
9. How will the father's messenger go by chariot to the ocean?
10. The mouse will not eat the lions.

Section I

Translate the following into Sanskrit:

One day a man is walking in the mountains. He sees a snake. He thinks, "I will hit the snake with (my) hand." He hits the snake. The snake falls from the tree and stands on the path. The man becomes frightened and runs from the snake to the sea. Suddenly Govinda shows the man the snake. The snake is in heaven. "Why is the snake in heaven?" asks the man. Govinda says, "You will go to heaven." For a long time the man lives in the world. But after a while he becomes dead. Govinda grabs <u>him</u> with (his) hand and places him in heaven.

frightened	भीतः	places	दधाति
dead	मृतः	him	तम्

11. THE SAGE AND THE MOUSE

I. *Vocabulary:* Learn the following words.

आगच्छति	he comes	व्याघ्रः	tiger
जानाति	he knows	अत्र	here
रक्षति	he protects	अनन्तरम्	immediately
आश्रमः	hermitage	पुनः	again
बिडालः	cat	नाम	by name

II *Grammar*:

The Past – अभवत्

(i) The Past Tense is formed in Sanskrit by adding अ to the front of the Stem, and the endings (as given below).

For example, चर-ति becomes अ-चर-त् ie अचरत्

(ii) Learn the following chart of the Past of भवति.

अभवत्	अभवताम्	अभवन्
he became	they two became	they became
अभवः	अभवतम्	अभवत
you became	you two became	you became
अभवम्	अभवाव	अभवाम
I became	we two became	we became

(iii) Past of Various क्रिया

Present	Meaning	Past	Meaning
वदति	says	अवदत्	said
पतति	falls	अपतत्	fell
चरति	walks	अचरत्	walked
पश्यति	sees	अपश्यत्	saw
तुदति	hits	अतुदत्	hit
चिन्तयति	thinks	अचिन्तयत्	thought
धावति	runs	अधावत्	ran
गच्छति	goes	अगच्छत्	went
आगच्छति	comes	आगच्छत्	came

III. *Syntax*:

1. The Past Tense

The Past Tense is used to express an action which happened in the Past.

For example: नरः अचरत्। The man walked.

नराः अचरन्। The men walked.

2. The Use of नाम to Name something

The word नाम is used in Sanskrit to mean 'by name'. It is placed after the name, as in English.

e.g. रामः नाम नरः वने वसति।

A man, Rāma by name, lives in the forest.

IV. ॥मुनिः मूषिकः च॥

1.आसीत् महातपा नाम मुनिः।

2.आश्रमे अवसत्।

3.आश्रमस्य समीपे क्षुधितम् मूषिकम् अपश्यत्।

4.तस्मात् मूषिकाय आहारम् अददात्।

5.मूषिकः बिडालम् अपश्यत्। भीतः अभवत्।

6.मुनिः अवदत् हे मूषिक बिडालः भव।

7.अनन्तरम् मूषिकः बिडालः अभवत्।

8.अन्यस्मिन् दिने बिडालः कुक्कुरम् अपश्यत्।

9.भीतः अभवत्।

10.तस्मात् मुनिम् अधावत्।

11.मुनिः मूषिकम् अपृच्छत् कुक्कुरात् बिभेषि। कुक्कुरः भव इति।

12.अनन्तरम् बिडालः कुक्कुरः अभवत्।

13.चिरेण व्याघ्रः आश्रमम् आगच्छत्।

14.कुक्कुरः व्याघ्रम् अपश्यत्।

15.भीतः अभवत्।

16.मुनिम् अधावत्।

17.मुनिः व्याघ्रम् अपश्यत्।

18.हे कुक्कुर व्याघ्रः भव इति अवदत्।

19.अनन्तरम् कुक्कुरः व्याघ्रः अभवत्।

20.चिरेण तु व्याघ्रः अचिन्तयत् मुनिः जानाति अहम् मूषिकः। तम् व्यापादयिष्यामि इति।

21.मुनिः व्याघ्रम् अपश्यत्।

22.सहसा व्याघ्रः तम् अधावत्।

23.पुनः अवदत् हे व्याघ्र मूषिकः भव इति।

24.तस्मात् व्याघ्रः पुनः मूषिकः अभवत्॥

Notes on Story 11

1.	आसीत्	there was
	महातपा	Mahātapā
	मुनिः	a sage
3.	आश्रमस्य समीपे	near the hermitage
	क्षुधितम्	hungry
4.	तस्मात्	therefore
	आहारः	food
5.	भीतः	afraid
6.	भव	become!
8.	अन्यस्मिन् दिने	on another day
10.	मुनिम्	to the sage
11.	कुक्कुरात् बिभेषि	are you afraid of the dog?
20.	अहम्	I am
	तम् व्यापादयिष्यामि	I will kill him
22.	तम्	to him
23.	पुनः	again

Chapter 11: Exercises

Section A

Write out all nine forms of the Past Tense of:

(a) चरति

(b) वदति

(c) गच्छति

Section B

State the Time when each of the following actions takes place: Present, Past or Future.

1. The men will run from the town to the house.
2. They ran to the boys.
3. You went to the house.
4. I will speak to the son of the king.
5. They give the present to the boys.
6. We will go to the city.
7. They are running to the house of the young man.
8. The two men saw the boy in the street.

Section C

Copy out the नाम *from the following sentences, and say which* विभक्ति *ending they should have; then, translate the sentences into Sanskrit.*

(i) We give the mouse to the man.
(ii) They ran from the hermitage.
(iii) We saw the men.
(iv) The snake went from the man's hermitage to the tree.
(v) The boys ran from the man.

Section D

(i) *State the Tense of each of the following,*
(ii) *Translate each.*

1. अधावन्
2. भविष्यसि
3. वदति
4. अपृच्छः
5. अपिबाम
6. अपश्यत्
7. अचरम्
8. गमिष्यसि
9. अतुदन्
10. चिन्तयन्ति

Section E

Translate the following into Sanskrit:

1. They saw
2. From the elephant
3. They will see
4. The son falls
5. The mouse will eat
6. I became
7. You will become
8. The man's dog
9. The elephant will walk
10. They asked
11. The messengers want
12. You think
13. We are running
14. The man stands
15. On the road
16. The men became
17. The boys ran
18. You will fall
19. The boy runs
20. The dog will run
21. We saw
22. They will think
23. He gives
24. The dogs will go
25. You (many) became
26. They grab
27. The mice ran
28. The dogs walked
29. The messengers sang
30. You will walk

Section F

Put the following into the Past, and then translate.

1. तुदति
2. चिन्तयतः
3. हरामः
4. पृच्छति
5. जीवसि
6. खादन्ति
7. धावतः
8. भवामि
9. गच्छावः
10. तिष्ठथ

Section G

Translate the following:

1. नरः बिडालम् अरक्षत्।
2. सहसा वृक्षः अपतत् इति अनन्तरम् दूतः वदति ।
3. आश्रमे मूषिकः अतिष्ठत्।
4. मूषिकम् बिडालाय न अददात् इति नराः वदिष्यन्ति।
5. कुतः वृक्षम् अगच्छः इति खगः कुक्कुरम् अपृच्छत्।
6. मार्गे चरिष्यामि इति व्याघ्रः अचिन्तयत्।
7. नित्यम् नरः आश्रमम् रथेन अगच्छत्।
8. सिंहः न स्वर्गे वसति इति जानामि।
9. सहसा नरः बालकम् हस्तेन अतुदत्।
10. नित्यम् कुक्कुरः मूषिकम् रक्षति इति नराः अवदन्।

Section H

Translate into Sanskrit:

1. The men ran from the trees to the mountains.
2. Immediately the messenger ran to the man.
3. The dog hears the roar of the lion.
4. The man stood in the hermitage.
5. The mouse saw the men in the trees.
6. The cat saw the dog.
7. A man, Rāma by name, lived here.
8. Suddenly the man hit the boy with a sword.
9. The man will go again to the hermitage
10. In the road the man hit the horse with his hand.

11A: THE LION'S MEAL

This is revision chapter, and can be passed over if time so dictates.

Revision of the Forms of भवति

Present

भवति	भवतः	भवन्ति
भवसि	भवथः	भवथ
भवामि	भवावः	भवामः

Future

भविष्यति	भविष्यतः	भविष्यन्ति
भविष्यसि	भविष्यथः	भविष्यथ
भविष्यामि	भविष्यावः	भविष्यामः

Past

अभवत्	अभवताम्	अभवन्
अभवः	अभवतम्	अभवत
अभवम्	अभवाव	अभवाम

।।सिंहस्य आहारः।।

1. एकदा सिंहः वने अचरत्।
2. सहसा शशकम् अपश्यत्।
3. अहम् क्षुधितः। शशकम् खादिष्यामि इति अचिन्तयत्।
4. अनन्तरम् शशकम् प्रति अधावत्।
5. सहसा तु मृगम् अपश्यत्।
6. मृगम् खादिष्यामि इति अचिन्तयत्।
7. अनन्तरम् मृगम् अन्वधावत्।
8. शीघ्रम् मृगः सिंहात् अधावत्।
9. सिंहः तु वृद्धः।
10. न शीघ्रम् धावितुम् अशक्नोत्।
11. तस्मात् मृगः अपाधावत्।
12. मृगम् न खादष्यािमि। इदानीम् तु शशकम् खादिष्यामि। शशकम् गमिष्यामि। यत्र शशकः वसति तत्र वृक्षः तिष्ठति। तत्र गमिष्यामि इति अचिन्तयत्।

13. सिंहः वृक्षम् अगच्छत्।

14. कुत्र तु शशकः।

15. शशकः अपाधावत्।

16. तस्मात् सिंहस्य न आहारः॥

Notes

3.	क्षुधितः	hungry
4.	प्रति *(after Accusative)*	towards
7.	अन्वधावत्	ran after
9.	वृद्धः	old
10.	धावितुम् अशक्नोत्	he was able to run
11.	अपाधावत्	he ran away
	यत्र	where
	तत्र	there

11A: Revision Exercises

Section A

Write out all nine forms of the Present, Future and Past of:

(a) गच्छति

(b) पश्यति

(c) चरति

Section B

State the Time when each of the following actions takes place: Present, Past or Future.

1. The boys went to the house of the man.
2. They will hit the man with the stick.
3. We see the men in the road.
4. The lions are eating the flesh of the dog.
5. You went to the house of the king.
6. You will see the dog of my master.

Section C

Copy out the नाम *from the following sentences, and say which* विभक्ति *ending they should have; then, translate the sentences into Sanskrit.*

(i) The lion is eating the food.
(ii) They were standing in the hermitage.
(iii) The man protects the dog.
(iv) The cat came from the house.
(v) The men will run away from the tiger.

Section D

Complete the following table, giving the Meaning, Present, Future and Past of each:

Meaning	Present	Future	Past
runs			
	पतति		
comes			
			अभवत्
sees			

Section E

(i) *State the Tense of each of the following.*
(ii) *Translate each.*

1. अचरन्
2. वदिष्यामः
3. गच्छन्ति
4. अगच्छताम्
5. तुदामि
6. अवदः
7. द्रक्ष्यसि
8. भवसि
9. गमिष्यति
10. रक्षन्ति

Section F

Translate the following into Sanskrit:

1. They will walk
2. You two see
3. They saw
4. By the men
5. With (his) hand
6. In the mountains
7. You will run
8. You are speaking
9. You two became
10. From a lion
11. He went
12. They will think
13. For the fathers
14. You give
15. He asked
16. They walked
17. By the dog
18. In the trees
19. They will run
20. We will go
21. By horse
22. They protect
23. They will dwell
24. He hears
25. For a man
26. They will eat
27. They walked
28. He conquered
29. We two drink
30. With a foot

Section G

Translate the following:

1. रथे रामः नरम् हस्तेन अतुदत्।
2. सहसा वृक्षाः अपतन्।
3. अचिरेण अचलम् गमिष्यामः इति दूतः अवदत्।
4. इदानीम् मृगः सूर्यम् पश्यति।
5. सिंहात् व्याघ्रात् च शीघ्रम् मूषिकः अधावत्।
6. कुत्र शशकस्य आहारः इति बालकः अपृच्छत्।
7. अहम् रामः इति नरः अवदत्।

8. खगाः वृक्षान् शीघ्रम् गमिष्यन्ति।
9. तत्र शशकः नित्यम् तिष्ठति।
10. इदानीम् कुत्र सूर्यः इति दूताः अपृच्छन्।

Section H

Translate into Sanskrit:

1. Where does the dog stand, O man?
2. The boys run quickly from the tigers.
3. The man protects the cat.
4. In the hermitage the boys are speaking again.
5. The cat saw the dogs, O Rāma.
6. The men will go to the trees soon.
7. A man, Rāma by name, went by chariot to the hermitage.
8. The rabbit and the deer were walking in the trees.
9. Now the rabbit wants food.
10. "We will see the sun soon," said the boy.

Section I

Translate into Sanskrit:

One day a man was walking in the trees. He saw a rabbit and thought, "I will eat the rabbit." Suddenly he saw a deer and thought, "I will eat the deer." The deer saw the man. He ran quickly away from the man. The rabbit ran away from the man. Therefore there was no food for the man!

there was आसीत् 'for': use the षष्ठी

12.THE BOY AND HIS BOOK

I. _Vocabulary:_ Learn the following words.

ज्ञानम्	knowledge	सत्यम्	truth
वनम्	forest	मित्रम्	friend
फलम्	fruit	नगरम्	city; town
पुष्पम्	flower	गृहम्	house
जलम्	water	पुस्तकम्	book

One उपनिषद् states:

सत्यम् ज्ञानम् अनन्तम् ब्रह्म।

Brahman is Truth, Knowledge, Infinite.

II _Grammar_:

Introduction to the Three लिङ्ग

In the world many things are divided by nature into male and female: in the case of humans, for example, there are men and women. There is a third class which is neither male nor female; a flower, for example, cannot be described as male or female, but has aspects of both. Sanskrit reflects this through what is called Gender or लिङ्ग. There are three लिङ्ग: Masculine, Feminine and Neuter. For example, Rāma is a man. Therefore the word रामः is Masculine. Sītā is a lady, and therefore her name is Feminine and so on.

There are Sanskrit words for Masculine, Feminine and Neuter. From this point onwards these will be used:

Masculine	पुंलिङ्ग	Feminine	स्त्रीलिङ्ग
Neuter	नपुंसकलिङ्ग		

All the नाम learnt so far in this course have ended in an अः (अ, followed by a विसर्ग). They are पुंलिङ्ग. Many नपुंसकलिङ्ग नाम end in अम्, and are declined like ज्ञानम्.

<u>ज्ञानम्</u>

ज्ञानम्	ज्ञाने	ज्ञानानि
हे ज्ञान	हे ज्ञाने	हे ज्ञानानि
ज्ञानम्	ज्ञाने	ज्ञानानि
ज्ञानेन	ज्ञानाभ्याम्	ज्ञानैः
ज्ञानाय	ज्ञानाभ्याम्	ज्ञानेभ्यः
ज्ञानात्	ज्ञानाभ्याम्	ज्ञानेभ्यः
ज्ञानस्य	ज्ञानयोः	ज्ञानानाम्
ज्ञाने	ज्ञानयोः	ज्ञानेषु

Notice that:

(i) the endings for ज्ञानम् differ only in the first nine forms from those for राम.

(ii) the endings for the द्वितीया विभक्ति are the same as those for the प्रथमा विभक्ति.

॥बालकः पुस्तकम् च॥

1. एकदा जनकः पुत्राय पुस्तकम् ददाति।
2. पुत्रः कृष्णकेशः नाम अस्ति।
3. वन्दनम् वन्दनम् हे जनक इति कृष्णकेशः वदति।
4. पुस्तकम् मित्रेभ्यः दर्शयिष्यामि इति वदति।
5. विद्यालयम् गच्छति।
6. विद्यालये कृष्णकेशः वदति हे मित्राणि। मम जनकः मह्यम् पुस्तकम् अददात् इति।
7. सर्वे बालकाः वदन्ति अस्मभ्यम् पुस्तकम् दर्शय इति।
8. पुस्तकम् पश्यन्ति।
9. अन्ततः कृष्णकेशः जनकस्य गृहम् गच्छति।
10. गृहे आहारम् खादति स्वप्नोति च।
11. प्रत्यूषे प्रबुद्धः भूत्वा विद्यालयम् पुनः गच्छति।
12. अत्र बालकाः वदन्ति अस्मभ्यम् तव पुस्तकम् दर्शय इति।

13. सहसा बालकः चिन्तयति कुत्र मम पुस्तकम्
अस्ति इति।

14. अनन्तरम् वदति हे मित्राणि कुत्र मम
पुस्तकम् अस्ति। युष्मासु चौरः अस्ति इति।

15. कृष्णकेशस्य वचनम् शृण्वन्ति वदन्ति च कः
चौरः अस्ति। कुत्र पुस्तकम् अस्ति इति।

16. तस्मात् गुरुः वदति कः चौरः अस्ति।
कुत्र पुस्तकम् अस्ति। यदि न कश्चित् वदति
अहम् चौरः अस्मि तर्हि सर्वान् शिष्यान्
दण्डयिष्यामि इति।

17. तस्मात् यदा न कश्चित् वदति अहम् चौरः
अस्मि। अत्र पुस्तकम् अस्ति इति तदा सर्वान्
शिष्यान् दण्डयति।

18. अन्ततः शिष्याः गृहाणि गच्छन्ति।

19. गृहे कृष्णकेशः चिन्तयति मम पुस्तकात् गुरुः
मम मित्राणि अदण्डयत् इति।

20. सहसा गृहे पुस्तकम् पश्यति।

21. हा हा मम पुस्तकम् नित्यम् अत्र आसीत्। अत्र तत् अत्यजम्। न चौरः अस्ति। गुरुः मम मित्राणि मम दोषात् अदण्डयत्। इदानीम् मित्राणि चिन्तयिष्यन्ति कृष्णकेशः न सत्यम् वदति। तस्य दोषात् गुरुः अस्मान् अदण्डयत् इति क्रोशति।

22. यतः बालकः एवम् व्यस्मरत् ततः गुरुः मित्राणि अदण्डयत्।

Notes

2.	अस्ति	is
5.	विद्यालयः	school
6.	मम	my
	मह्यम्	to me
7.	सर्वे	all
	अस्मभ्यम्	to us
	दर्शय	show *(gives an instruction)*
9.	अन्ततः	in the end; finally
10.	स्वप्नोति	sleeps
11.	प्रत्यूषे	in the morning
	प्रबुद्धः	awake
	भूत्वा	having become
12.	तव	your
14.	युष्मासु	amongst you
	चौरः	a thief
15.	वचनम्	word; statement
	शृण्वन्ति	they hear
	कः	who
16.	गुरुः	teacher
	यदि	if
	न कश्चित्	no one
	अस्मि	I am
	तर्हि	then
	सर्वान्	all
	शिष्यः	a pupil
17.	यदा	when
	तदा	then
19.	पुस्तकात्	*the* पञ्चमी *can mean "because of"*
21.	हा हा	Alas! Alas!
	आसीत्	was
	तत्	it
	दोषः	fault; mistake
	तस्य	his
	अस्मान्	us
22.	यतः	since
	एवम्	in this way
	व्यस्मरत्	(he) forgot
	ततः	therefore

Chapter 12: Exercises

Section A

Translate the following into Sanskrit:

1. In a house
2. Away from the trees
3. They will go
4. The fruits
5. He ran
6. In a book
7. He saw
8. Of the town
9. From the water
10. The books fell
11. He walks in the forest
12. They eat in the city
13. The fruit falls
14. He will go to the house
15. The boy goes to town
16. In knowledge
17. To the city
18. We shall walk
19. From the forest
20. You two drank
21. For water
22. By a friend
23. Of the flowers
24. In the books
25. They grab the flowers
26. You run to the town
27. The friends run to the house
28. They are drinking water
29. Truth does not go
30. The men will eat the fruits

Section B

State the लिङ्ग *of the* नाम *in the following sentences:*

1. The man hits the boy.
2. The girls talk to their fathers.
3. The boys see the ships.
4. We will go to the old man.
5. The children are not nearby.

Section C

Say whether each of the following is पुंलिङ्ग *or* नपुंसकलिङ्ग.

1. गृहम्
2. ज्ञानाय
3. अश्वान्
4. जलम्
5. फलानि
6. स्वर्गस्य
7. रामस्य
8. ज्ञानम्
9. पुष्पाणि
10. अचलयोः
11. मित्राणाम्
12. सत्यम्

Section D

Translate the following:

1. बालकः नित्यम् सत्यम् वदति।
2. बालकाः गृहम् धावन्ति इति नरः अवदत्।
3. नराः बालकाः च वनम् न गमिष्यन्ति।
4. सिंहः मृगम् शशकान् च वने अपश्यत्।
5. दूताः जलम् शीघ्रम् अपिबन्।
6. दूतस्य गृहे मूषिकः वसति।
7. मित्रम् बालकम् हस्तेन न अतुदत् इति चिन्तयति।
8. कुतः नगरम् न अगच्छः इति नरः अपृच्छत्।
9. सहसा फलम् वृक्षात् अपतत्।
10. इदानीम् कुत्र सूर्यः इति नरः अपृच्छत्।

Section E

Translate into Sanskrit:

1. The tiger came to the man's house.
2. The man immediately went to the forest.
3. The boys eat the food quickly.
4. The fruit of the tree fell.
5. The water falls from the trees.
6. The friends will go to the city.
7. "I will eat the boy's food," thinks the rabbit.
8. "We will run from the house to the forest," said the men.
9. The messenger gives truth and knowledge to the boys.
10. Immediately the lions and the tigers saw the sun.

Section F

Translate into Sanskrit:

One day a man was walking in the forest. He saw a deer and a rabbit. Suddenly he saw a lion. "O Govinda," he said, "why do you not protect <u>me</u>? The lion <u>will kill</u> me." Govinda heard <u>those words</u>. Immediately the lion ran away from the man. The man walked quickly to (his) house.

me = माम्

kills = व्यापादयति

those words = तानि वचनानि

13. THE ELEPHANT COMES TO TOWN

I. *Vocabulary:* Learn the following words.

नासिका	nose	शय्या	bed
तारका	star	सेना	army
पेटा	box	नौका	boat
भार्या	wife	आस्यम्	mouth
शाला	room	स्पृशति	touches

II *Grammar*:

Many स्त्रीलिङ्ग, or Feminine, नाम in Sanskrit end in an आ. The name of Rāma's wife, Sītā, is used as an example.

सीता

सीता	सीते	सीताः
हे सीते	हे सीते	हे सीताः
सीताम्	सीते	सीताः
सीतया	सीताभ्याम्	सीताभिः
सीतायै	सीताभ्याम्	सीताभ्यः
सीतायाः	सीताभ्याम्	सीताभ्यः
सीतायाः	सीतयोः	सीतानाम्
सीतायाम्	सीतयोः	सीतासु

III. *Syntax*:

Making a Comparison

The word इव means 'like'. It is written after the descriptive word in a comparison or simile, *e.g.* 'The boy was like a cat.' = 'The boy was cat-like.' In Sanskrit it is always in this order:

For example: रामः सिंहः इव अधावत्।

Rāma ran like a lion.

नरः व्याघ्रः इव वनम् अगच्छत्।

The man went like a tiger to the forest.

IV. ॥गजः नगरम् आगच्छति॥

1. एकदा एकः गजः नगरम् आगच्छत्।
2. नगरे बहवः जनाः अवसन्।
3. नगरे तु न कश्चित् द्रष्टुम् अशक्नोत्।
4. सर्वे अन्धाः आसन्।
5. यदा गजः नगरम् आगच्छत् तदा सर्वे तम् अगच्छन्।
6. प्रथमः नरः गजस्य पादम् अस्पर्शत्।
7. गजः स्तम्भः इव अस्ति इति अवदत्।
8. द्वितीयः नरः गजस्य नासिकाम् अस्पर्शत्।
9. गजः सर्पः इव अस्ति इति अवदत्।
10. तृतीयः नरः गजस्य आस्यम् अस्पर्शत्।
11. गजः शूर्पम् इव अस्ति इति अवदत्।
12. इदम् गजः अस्ति। तत् गजः अस्ति इति सर्वे जनाः अवदन्।
13. किम् तु गजः अस्ति।

1.	एकः	a certain
2.	बहवः	many
3.	न कश्चित्	no one
	द्रष्टुम्	to see
	अशक्नोत्	was able
4.	सर्वे	all
	अन्धाः	blind
	आसन्	they were
5.	यदा	when
	तदा	then
	तम्	to him
6.	प्रथमः	the first
	अस्पर्शत्	he touched
7.	अस्ति	is
	स्तम्भः	post; pillar
8.	द्वितीयः	the second
10.	तृतीयः	the third
11.	शूर्पम्	basket
12.	इदम्	this
	तत्	that
13.	किम्	what?

Chapter 13: Exercises

Section A

State the लिङ्ग *of the following:*

1. शय्या
2. ज्ञानम्
3. पेटा
4. बालकः
5. पुस्तकम्
6. रामः
7. नौका
8. सत्यम्
9. तारका
10. नरः

Section B

Translate the following into Sanskrit:

1. From the stars
2. They will see
3. With two men
4. By the truth
5. For the lady
6. We will run
7. On a box
8. In the house
9. He sees
10. You two are running
11. To the dogs
12. Let them dwell
13. In heaven
14. In the army
15. In the flowers
16. In the bed
17. He became
18. In a boat
19. From knowledge
20. They two will hit
21. They will speak
22. From books
23. To the house
24. The men think
25. From the lions
26. In the chariot
27. From the stars
28. For the wife
29. In the boxes
30. From the city

Section C

Translate the following:

1. हे बालक। कुतः पेटायाम् तिष्ठसि इति अवदत्।
2. शालाम् गमिष्यामः इति मित्रम् इव अवदत्।
3. नराः भार्याः च नगरम् आगमिष्यन्ति।
4. सिंहाः व्याघ्राः इव नित्यम् शशकान् खादन्ति।
5. जनकस्य गृहे बालकाः नित्यम् वसन्ति।
6. अनन्तरम् भार्या बालकम् हस्तेन अतुदत्।
7. बालकः जनकस्य नौकाम् अपश्यत्।
8. नगरम् रथैः गमिष्यन्ति इति भार्याः चिन्तयन्ति।
9. सहसा नरः अवदत् हे मित्र। कथम् भार्या वदिष्यति इति।
10. इदानीम् मृगाः शशकाः इव तारकाम् न पश्यन्ति।

Section D

Translate the following into Sanskrit:

1. "Soon we will see the man's house," said the wife.
2. The man will come like a tiger to the boat.
3. An army came quickly from the forest.
4. Suddenly the wife saw the snake.
5. Soon the army will come to the city.
6. O wife, look at the stars in heaven.
7. The man protects the boys like a father.
8. The cat sees the mouse in the box.
9. "We will run to the house, friends," said the man's wife.
10. The mouse ran quickly from the cat.

14. THE SAGE AND THE BOY

I. *Vocabulary:* Learn the following words.

अनेक	many	ज्येष्ठ°	eldest
अरुण°	red	दीर्घ°	long
अल्प°	small	प्राज्ञ°	wise
उत्तम°	best; highest	वीर°	brave
उन्नत°	tall	शान्त°	peaceful
कुपित°	angry	शुद्ध°	pure
कृष्ण°	black	प्रिय°	dear

II. *Grammar*:

Describing Things - विशेषण।

Languages are often used to describe things. Indeed, a नाम or क्रिया is giving a description of a thing or event by assigning a name to it. A नाम on its own, though, may not tell the whole story. For example, "A man is walking down the street." What do we know of this man, apart from what he is doing? We do not know anything of the qualities of the man. If we wished to know, we might well ask, "What sort of man?" "A great man is walking down the street", or "A wise man is walking down the street." We can now say something about the man's qualities, and describe him further. Such words are called "Adjectives" or विशेषण in grammar, and bring out qualities which would otherwise remain hidden.

<u>Definition of a विशेषण</u>

A विशेषण is a word which brings out a quality of someone or something.

In Sanskrit, a विशेषण has to take the same लिङ्ग, विभक्ति ending and वचन as the नाम which it is describing. Hence the little circle after each विशेषण in the vocabulary, which shows that we have to add the appropriate ending. The following table shows all the forms of शान्त° in पुंलिङ्ग, स्त्रीलिङ्ग and नपुंसकलिङ्ग.

The Forms of विशेषण

पुंलिङ्ग			स्त्रीलिङ्ग			नपुंसकलिङ्ग		
शान्तः	शान्तौ	शान्ताः	शान्ता	शान्ते	शान्ताः	शान्तम्	शान्ते	शान्तानि
शान्त	शान्तौ	शान्ताः	शान्ते	शान्ते	शान्ताः	शान्त	शान्ते	शान्तानि
शान्तम्	शान्तौ	शान्तान्	शान्ताम्	शान्ते	शान्ताः	शान्तम्	शान्ते	शान्तानि
शान्तेन	शान्ताभ्याम्	शान्तैः	शान्तया	शान्ताभ्याम्	शान्ताभिः	शान्तेन	शान्ताभ्याम्	शान्तैः
शान्ताय	शान्ताभ्याम्	शान्तेभ्यः	शान्तायै	शान्ताभ्याम्	शान्ताभ्यः	शान्ताय	शान्ताभ्याम्	शान्तेभ्यः
शान्तात्	शान्ताभ्याम्	शान्तेभ्यः	शान्तायाः	शान्ताभ्याम्	शान्ताभ्यः	शान्तात्	शान्ताभ्याम्	शान्तेभ्यः
शान्तस्य	शान्तयोः	शान्तानाम्	शान्तायाः	शान्तयोः	शान्तानाम्	शान्तस्य	शान्तयोः	शान्तानाम्
शान्ते	शान्तयोः	शान्तेषु	शान्तायाम्	शान्तयोः	शान्तासु	शान्ते	शान्तयोः	शान्तेषु

III. <u>Syntax</u>:

1. Agreement of नाम and विशेषण

There is a form of a विशेषण to agree with any form of any नाम in Sanskrit. They must agree in the following three aspects: लिङ्ग, विभक्ति and वचन. Often this means that the ending of the विशेषण is the same as that of the नाम, but this is not always the case, so care is needed.

For example,

The eldest son runs to the black dog:
ज्येष्ठः पुत्रः कृष्णम् कुक्कुरम् धावति।

The brave man sees (his) peaceful wife:
वीरः नरः शान्ताम् भार्याम् पश्यति।

2. 'Together With'

The word सह means 'together with'. It is used with the तृतीया विभक्ति. It is written after the word in the तृतीया विभक्ति.

For example:

रामेण सह	together with Rāma
सीतया सह	together with Sītā

॥ऋषिः बालकः च॥

1. एकदा एकः प्राज्ञः ऋषिः आसीत्।

2. वने अवसत्।

3. तेन सह गृहे बालकः अवसत्।

4. बालकः नित्यम् ऋषेः साहाय्यम् अकरोत्।

5. एकदा ऋषिः अवदत् किम् इच्छसि बालक इति।

6. अहम् शान्तः सन्तुष्टः च। मम तु जनकः मृतः अभवत्। न मुक्तः अभवत्। नित्यम् स्वप्नेषु माम् आगच्छति इति बालकः अवदत्।

7. तानि वचनानि ऋषिः अशृणोत्।

8. पीडितः अभवत्।

9. किम् करिष्यामि इति पुनः पुनः अचिन्तयत्।

10. एकदा बालकः नगरम् अगच्छत्।

11. तस्मात् शय्यायाम् न अस्वपात्।

12. ऋषिः शय्याम् अगच्छत्।

13. शय्यायाम् अचिन्तयत् किम् मया कर्तव्यम्। बालकस्य जनकः न मुक्तः अभवत्। तस्मात्

न शान्तः अभवत्। बालकस्य तु साहाय्यम् कर्तुम् इच्छामि इति।

14.ऋषिः अस्वपात्।

15.नगरात् बालकः गृहम् आगच्छत्।

16.वातायनेन गृहम् प्राविशत्।

17.शय्यायाम् अस्वपात्।

18.प्रातः ऋषिः शय्याम् अत्यजत्।

19.बालकस्य शय्यायाम् शरीरम् अपश्यत्।

20.अहो अहो तत्र बालकस्य जनकः इति अचिन्तयत्।

21.भीतः अभवत्।

22.शीघ्रम् शरीरात् धाविष्यामि इति अचिन्तयत्।

23.तस्मात् वातायनेन प्लवनम् अकरोत्।

24.शब्दम् श्रुत्वा बालकः अचिन्तयत् चौरः गृहम् आगच्छत् इति।

25.लगुडम् अहरत्।

26.ऋषिम् लगुडेन अतुदत्।

27.बालक। हे बालक। कुतः माम् तुदसि। मा मित्रम् तुद इति ऋषिः अवदत्।

28.अन्ते मार्गे ऋषिम् अपश्यत्।

1.	एकः	a certain
	ऋषिः	sage
	आसीत्	there was
3.	तेन	him (तृतीया विभक्ति)
4.	ऋषेः साहाय्यम् अकरोत्	he helped the sage
5.	किम्	What?
6.	सन्तुष्ट°	content
	मृत°	dead
	मुक्त°	liberated
	स्वप्नः	sleep; dream
	माम्	to me
7.	तानि वचनानि	those words
8.	पीडित°	distressed
9.	करिष्यामि	I will do
11.	अस्वपात्	he slept
13.	किम् मया कर्तव्यम्	What must I do?
	साहाय्यम् कर्तुम्	to help
16.	वातायनेन	through the window

	प्राविशत्	entered
18.	प्रातः	early
19.	शरीरम्	a body
21.	भीत०	afraid
23.	प्लवनम् अकरोत्	he plunged
24.	शब्दः	sound
	श्रुत्वा	having heard
	चौरः	thief
25.	लगुडः	a stick
	ऋषिम्	the sage
27.	मा	do not
	तदु	hit
28.	अन्ते	in the end; finally

Chapter 14 Exercises:

Section A

Add the correct ending to each विशेषण.

1. कुपित नरः
2. अल्प गजम्
3. उन्नत नरात्
4. कृष्ण गजस्य
5. प्राज्ञ नराणाम्
6. उन्नत वृक्षे
7. उत्तम व्याघ्राः
8. प्रिय पुत्रयोः
9. वीर मत्स्यानाम्
10. कुपित मित्राणि
11. अरुण अश्वस्य
12. कुपित भार्यया
13. शुद्ध नराय
14. दीर्घ नासिकासु
15. कृष्ण पेटायाम्
16. अल्प नरस्य
17. शान्त वनम्
18. दीर्घ मार्गे
19. प्राज्ञ खगस्य
20. अल्प पेटायाम्

Section B

Translate the following into Sanskrit:

1. By the tall man
2. From the peaceful man
3. On the black horse
4. You (many) went
5. To the angry men
6. You will walk
7. From the black snakes
8. The black books
9. Of the eldest son
10. In the long story
11. In the red box
12. They will run
13. In the tall trees
14. For the best son
15. Of the pure wives
16. In the peaceful hermitage
17. He hit the angry friend
18. In the red book
19. From the peaceful house
20. From the brave army

Section C

Translate the following:

1. कुपितः नरः अल्पाम् सेनाम् अपश्यत्।
2. शुद्धाः बालकाः नित्यम् सत्यम् वदन्ति।
3. ज्येष्ठः पुत्रः वनम् गमिष्यति इति प्राज्ञः नरः चिन्तयति।
4. कृष्णः खगः नरेण सह गृहात् अगच्छत्।
5. वीराः नराः कृष्णम् खगम् अतुदन्।
6. उन्नतः नरः शीघ्रम् अरुणात् गृहात् अधावत्।
7. उत्तमे गृहे कृष्णः बिडालः नरेण सह अवसत्।
8. कुपिताः व्याघ्राः सिंहाः च नरान् अखादन्।
9. अनन्तरम् रामः नाम वीरः नरः भार्यया सह शान्तात् आश्रमात् शीघ्रम् अधावत्।
10. प्राज्ञः नरः अल्पान् शशकान् न खादिष्यति इति बालकाः अचिन्तयन्।

Section D

Translate the following into Sanskrit:

1. The son goes to (his) father's house together with (his) friends.
2. The brave man did not see the black snake.
3. "I will not strike the peaceful man," the tall man thought.
4. In the small forest the friends hit the deer with (their) hands.
5. The eldest man stood on a red box together with (his) wife.
6. The brave man went in the small boat to the city.
7. The boys ran from the angry lion to the small boat.
8. The peaceful man stood in the boy's boat together with (his) sons.
9. The tall man saw (his) angry wife.
10. They went to the small town and saw the man's red dog.

15. THE DOG, THE DONKEY AND THE THIEF

I. *Vocabulary*:

चौरः	thief	आनयति	brings
गर्दभः	donkey	अतीव	very
लगुडः	stick	घोर॰	horrible
पीठम्	chair	प्रबल॰	powerful
द्वीपः	island	कदा	when?

II. *Grammar*:

The सर्वनाम तत्

In Sanskrit, as in English, there are words for 'he', 'she', 'it' and 'they'. Such words are called Pronouns or सर्वनाम, because they may stand in the place of any नाम. Indeed, the word सर्वनाम means 'a name for all'. Like any नाम, they have a full range of विभक्ति, एकवचन, द्विवचन and बहुवचन and three लिङ्ग.

One such is तत् which means 'he', 'she', 'it' or 'that'.

Take care when learning its forms, as they are not all the same as those which you have met before.

Note also that there are no संबोधन forms of तत्.

The Forms of तत्

पुंलिङ्ग			स्त्रीलिङ्ग			नपुंसकलिङ्ग		
सः	तौ	ते	सा	ते	ताः	तत्	ते	तानि
तम्	तौ	तान्	ताम्	ते	ताः	तत्	ते	तानि
तेन	ताभ्याम्	तैः	तया	ताभ्याम्	ताभिः	तेन	ताभ्याम्	तैः
तस्मै	ताभ्याम्	तेभ्यः	तस्यै	ताभ्याम्	ताभ्यः	तस्मै	ताभ्याम्	तेभ्यः
तस्मात्	ताभ्याम्	तेभ्यः	तस्याः	ताभ्याम्	ताभ्यः	तस्मात्	ताभ्याम्	तेभ्यः
तस्य	तयोः	तेषाम्	तस्याः	तयोः	तासाम्	तस्य	तयोः	तेषाम्
तस्मिन्	तयोः	तेषु	तस्याम्	तयोः	तासु	तस्मिन्	तयोः	तेषु

III. <u>*Syntax*</u>:

The Use of तत्

In English there are a number different forms of the words 'he, she and it'. Note the following examples:

तस्य गृहम्	His house
तस्याः गृहम्	Her house
तम् पश्यति	He sees him.
ताम् पश्यति	He sees her.
ताः पश्यति	They see them.
तासाम् पुस्तकम्	Their book

It may be helpful to look through these examples, and identify the forms in Sanskrit on the table (on the previous page). Many other forms have not been listed, and a thorough study of the English of this paradigm can avoid problems with the exercises.

॥गर्दभः कुक्कुरः चौरः च॥

आसीत् कर्पूरपटकः नाम नरः। एकदा चौरः तस्य गृहम् आगच्छत्। गृहस्य प्राङ्गणे बद्धः गर्दभः कुक्कुरः च अतिष्ठताम्। गर्दभः चौरम् अपश्यत्। सः कुक्कुरम् अवदत् हे कुक्कुर गृहम् चौरः प्रविशति। अपि तम् न पश्यसि। गृहम् रक्ष इति। न किंचित् करिष्यामि। नित्यम् अहम् क्षुधितः। कर्पूरपटकः न मह्यम् आहारम् ददाति। न किंचित् करिष्यामि इति कुक्कुरः अवदत्। गर्दभः प्राङ्गणे कुक्कुरम् पुनः अवदत् गच्छ। चौरम् प्रति धाव इति। न किंचित् इति कुक्कुरः अवदत्। गर्दभः नादम् अकरोत्। चौरः शीघ्रम् गृहात् अधावत्। गृहे तु नरः नादेन प्रबुद्धः कुपितः गृहात् अधावत्। गर्दभम् लगुडेन अतुदत्। गर्दभः लगुडेन मृतः अभवत्॥

Notes

अकरोत्	he made
अपि	*makes a question (do you not...?)*
आसीत्	there was
करिष्यति	he will do
किंचित्	anything; something
क्षुधित०	hungry
प्रति	towards (with द्वितीया)
प्रबुद्ध०	awoken
प्रविशति	he enters
प्राङ्गणम्	courtyard
बद्ध०	bound
मह्यम्	to/for me
हत०	dead

The Vocbulary for this and subsequent stories is given in the order in which it appears in the Sanskrit Dictionary, not by sentence.

Chapter 15 Exercises

Section A

(i) *Give the* विभक्ति, वचन *and* लिङ्ग *of each of the following;*
(ii) *Then translate.*

1. तत्	6. तस्मिन्	11. सा
2. ते	7. तयोः	12. ताः
3. तम्	8. तासाम्	13. सः
4. तौ	9. तेषु	14. तेन
5. तस्य	10. तेभ्यः	15. तस्मै

Section B

Give each of the following forms of तत्

1.	चतुर्थी	एकवचन	स्त्रीलिङ्ग
2.	पञ्चमी	द्विवचन	पुंलिङ्ग
3.	षष्ठी	बहुवचन	पुंलिङ्ग
4.	सप्तमी	बहुवचन	नपुंसकलिङ्ग
5.	प्रथमा	एकवचन	नपुंसकलिङ्ग
6.	द्वितीया	द्विवचन	स्त्रीलिङ्ग
7.	तृतीया	बहुवचन	पुंलिङ्ग
8.	प्रथमा	द्विवचन	स्त्रीलिङ्ग
9.	तृतीया	एकवचन	पुंलिङ्ग
10.	सप्तमी	एकवचन	स्त्रीलिङ्ग

Section C

Give the correct endings for each विशेषण *in the following:*

1. वीर नरस्य
2. अल्प वृक्षे
3. घोर लगुडेन
4. कृष्ण सर्पः
5. शुद्ध नरौ
6. प्रबल नारी
7. अरुण पीठानाम्
8. उत्तम नौकायाम्
9. प्रिय बालकात्
10. प्राज्ञ गजैः

Section D

Translate the following:

1. अरुणे पीठे सा अतिष्ठत्।
2. वीरः नरः घोरम् चौरम् तस्मात् आनयति।
3. सा नित्यम् द्वीपे वसति।
4. कदा तत् अवदम् हे नर।
5. प्रबलाः बालकाः तैः गर्दभम् तोत्स्यन्ति।
6. कदा सः कुपितम् चौरम् अपश्यत् इति सीता अपृच्छत्।
7. तेन तम् अतुदम् इति सा अवदत्।
8. शुद्धाः प्राज्ञाः च नराः नित्यम् तानि खादन्ति।
9. अतीव अल्पः खगः शान्तम् नगरम् गच्छति।
10. द्वीपे प्रबलम् सिंहम् ताः अपश्यन्।

Section E

Translate the following into Sanskrit:

1. She stands on the horrible island.
2. The horrible man hit him with a stick.
3. The powerful man saw her in the boat.
4. They did not run away from the very powerful thieves.
5. "When did you see him?" asked the angry king.
6. The tall man was walking with them.
7. The brave man saw the small, red snake.
8. The eldest son of the king did not hit her.
9. They went by a long road to the small town.
10. "I will eat it," thought the wise man.

16. THE MAN AND THE LION

I. *Vocabulary:* Learn the following words.

आहारः	food	तत्र	there
शशकः	rabbit	कुत्र	where?
मृगः	deer	तस्मात्	therefore
सूर्यः	sun	इदानीम्	now
अहम्	I (am)	शीघ्रम्	quickly

II *Grammar*:

The Imperative - लोट्

भवतु Let him be!	भवताम् Let those two be!	भवन्तु Let them be!
भव Be!	भवतम् (You two) be!	भवत (You many) be!
भवानि Let me be!	भवाव Let us two be!	भवाम Let us be!

III. <u>*Syntax*</u>:

1. The Uses of The Imperative - लोट्

All the forms of क्रिया used so far in the course have *indicated* an action which is taking place in the Present, will take place in the Future or has taken place in the Past. Such forms are called *Indicative*. It is also necessary to express actions in other ways. Sometimes, for example, one might need to tell someone what to do or give them a command. The *Imperative*, called लोट् in Sanskrit Grammar, is used to give a command. The word '*Imperative*' comes from the Latin *imperare*, to order.

For example: तूष्णीम् भव। Be silent!

Note that, as in English, the प्रथमपुरुष and मध्यमपुरुष are frequently used, but the उत्तमपुरुष only very rarely.

2. Prohibitions

To make a prohibition, or negative command, the word मा is used with लोट्. न is not used.

For example:

बालकाः मा गृहे धावत। Boys, do not run in the house!

3. अहम्

The word अहम् can mean 'I am' or simply 'I'.

One of the most famous statements in Sanskrit is:

अहम् ब्रह्मास्मि। I am Brahman.

IV. ।।नरः सिंहः च।।

1.एकदा नरः मार्गे अचरत्।

2.सहसा सिंहम् अपश्यत्।

3.हा हा किम् करिष्यामि। मार्गे सिंहम् पश्यामि इति अवदत्।

4.अन्यम् नरम् अपश्यत्।

5.हे नर। सिंहः मार्गे तिष्ठति। माम् खादिष्यति। किम् करिष्यामि। अत्र आगच्छ। माम् रक्ष इति अक्रोशत्।

6.तस्य वचनानि तु नरः न अशृणोत्।

7.सिंहः नरम् अपश्यत्।

8.अहम् आहारम् इच्छामि। तस्मात् नरम् खादिष्यामि इति अचिन्तयत्।

9.तस्मात् सिंहः अनन्तरम् अखादत्।

10.अन्यस्मिन् दिने प्राज्ञः नरः मार्गे सिंहम् अपश्यत्।

11.सिंहः नरम् अपश्यत्।

12.अहम् आहारम् इच्छामि। तस्मात् नरम् खादिष्यामि इति अचिन्तयत्।

13.अहम् ब्रह्म अस्मि। सर्वम् हि एतत् ब्रह्म इति प्राज्ञः नरः अचिन्तयत्।

14.ईश्वरः सिंहस्य रूपे आत्मानम् मा दर्शयतु इति अवदत्।

15.सहसा सिंहः बिडालः अभवत्।

16.अनन्तरम् बिडालः नरात् अधावत्।

Notes

अन्यम्	another
अन्यस्मिन् दिने	on another day
अस्मि	I am
अशृणोत्	he heard
आत्मानम्	(your) Self
ईश्वरः	Lord
एतत्	this
किम् करिष्यामि	What will I do?
क्रोशति	he cries out
तस्य वचनानि	his words
माम्	me
प्राज्ञः	wise
ब्रह्म	Brahman
सर्वम्	all
रूपम्	form
हा हा	Alas! Alas!
हि	for *(translate first)*

Chapter 16: Exercises

Section A

Translate the following:

1. गच्छ
2. चरतु
3. भव
4. चिन्तयताम्
5. चराम
6. पश्य
7. भवाम
8. चरन्तु
9. मा भवाव
10. चिन्तय
11. भवतु
12. तिष्ठ
13. चरन्तु
14. धावत
15. मा धाव
16. वदतम्
17. मा भव
18. वदाव
19. मा चरत
20. मा गच्छ

Section B

Translate the following into Sanskrit:

1. Run!
2. Let him think!
3. Do not run! (pl.)
4. Do not see!
5. Let us speak!
6. Let them not become (pl.)!
7. Go!
8. Don't think! (pl.)
9. Do not walk!
10. Do not hit the man with (your) hand!
11. Do not speak!
12. (You two) Do not run!
13. Stand!
14. Be quiet!
15. Do not let them go!

Section C

Translate the following into English:

1. हे बालक मा रामम् गच्छ इति नरः अवदत्।
2. हे नर मा गजम् हस्तेन तुद इति खगः वदिष्यति।
3. हे मृगाः वृक्षात् शीघ्रम् धावत इति वदामि।
4. तस्मात् मा नरः तत्र तिष्ठतु।
5. इदानीम् कुत्र चरसि हे शशक मा आहारम् त्यज।
6. हे भार्ये इदानीम् नरम् गच्छ पृच्छ च।
7. सूर्यात् शीघ्रम् पतत हे खगाः।
8. हे बालकौ आहारम् खादतम्।
9. नित्यम् वन्दनम् वन्दनम् हे नर इति वद हे बालक।
10. आश्रमे दूताः नित्यम् बिडालम् रक्षन्तु इति वदतु।

Section D

Translate the following into Sanskrit:

1. "Do not go to the tree, boys," said the man.
2. Always run from the hermitage, boys.
3. Let men live and walk in the world.
4. Now ask the man, "Where is the hermitage?"
5. Let the cat eat the mouse.
6. Let him ask the messenger, "Where have I left the food?"
7. The boys will say, "Let them not see the dogs and cats."
8. Let him go to the messenger and ask, "Where will you walk, o man?
9. Do not go there, boys.
10. Let them see the fishes in the sea.

17. THE THIEVES, THE BRĀHMAṆA AND THE GOAT

I. *Vocabulary*:

छागः	goat	किमिति	why?
दुर्जनः	an evil man	किंतु	but
यज्ञः	sacrifice	भोः	O!
ब्राह्मणः	Brāhmaṇa	अन्य०	other; another
स्कन्धः	shoulder	समीपे	near, in the presence of (षष्ठी)

II. *Grammar*:

1. The Past Active Participle (Gerund)

The Past Active Participle is a form of a क्रिया which ends in त्वा. It means 'having (done an action)...' It is formed by adding त्वा or sometimes इत्वा to the धातु.

Learn the following table of Past Active Participle forms.

पतति	पतित्वा	having fallen
धावति	धावित्वा	having run
चरति	चरित्वा	having walked
खादति	खादित्वा	having eaten
त्यजति	त्यक्त्वा	having left/abandoned
भवति	भूत्वा	having become
गच्छति	गत्वा	having gone
शृणोति	श्रुत्वा	having heard
पश्यति	दृष्ट्वा	having seen

2. Other - अन्य०

The forms of अन्य० are like those of तत्.

For example,

अन्यस्मिन् नरे = on another man

अन्ये नराः चरन्ति। = Other men walk

III. Syntax:

1. The Use of The Past Active Participle

All the forms of क्रिया which we have used so far can be used to form a sentence, without adding anything else.

For example, अधावत्, he ran.

There are, however, other forms which do not make a complete sentence on their own, and they need a main क्रिया to complete the sentence. For example, 'having run to the town' is not a sentence. To complete the sentence, we might say, 'Having run to the town, he saw his wife.'

The Past Active Participles mean 'having done an action...' and cannot make a complete sentence. The following sentences are examples of their use:

रामम् दृष्ट्वा नारी वनम् अगच्छत्।

Having seen Rāma, the lady went to the forest.

तत् श्रुत्वा रामः वनम् अगच्छत्।

Having heard that, Rāma went to the forest.

Notice that the त्वा ending is unchanging whatever the Subject.

2. तत् - That

The forms of तत् can be used to agree with a नाम to mean 'that' or 'those'. Like a विशेषण they must have the same लिङ्ग, विभक्ति and वचन as the नाम with which they are used.

For example:	सः नरः।	that man
	तानि वचनानि।	those words.
	तम् वृक्षम् अपश्यम्।	I saw that tree.

3. Near - समीपे

समीपे means 'near' or 'in the presence of'. It is used with a word in the षष्ठी which comes before it.

For example, वृक्षस्य समीपे = near a tree.

॥चौराः ब्रह्मणः छागः च॥

एकदा वने ब्राह्मणः यज्ञम् अकरोत्। सः नगरम् अगच्छत्। नगरे यज्ञार्थम् छागम् उपक्रीय स्कन्धे धृत्वा वनम् अचरत्। तम् त्रयः दुर्जनाः अपश्यन्। ते अचिन्तयन् तम् छागम् इच्छामः इति। तस्मात् प्रथमः दुर्जनः मार्गम् गत्वा वृक्षस्य समीपे अतिष्ठत्। ब्राह्मणम् दृष्ट्वा अपृच्छत् भोः ब्राह्मण। किमिति कुक्कुरः स्कन्धेन उह्यते इति। तम् ब्राह्मणः अवदत् न कुक्कुरः। किंतु यज्ञच्छागः इति। द्वितीयः दुर्जनः अन्यस्य वृक्षस्य समीपे अतिष्ठत्। ब्राह्मणम् दृष्ट्वा अपृच्छत् भोः ब्राह्मण। किमिति कुक्कुरः स्कन्धेन उह्यते इति। तम् ब्राह्मणः अवदत् न कुक्कुरः। किंतु यज्ञच्छागः इति। तस्मात् तृतीयम् नरम् ब्राह्मणः अमिलत्। सः अपृच्छत् किमिति कुक्कुरः स्बन्धेन उह्यते इति। तत् श्रुत्वा ब्राह्मणः अचिन्तयत् किम् करोमि। अयम् न छागः। अयम् कुक्कुरः इति। छागम् त्यक्त्वा नगरम् पुनः अचरत्। अनन्तरम् दुर्जनाः छागम् गृहीत्वा शीघ्रम् अखादन्।

Notes:

अमिलत्	he met
अयम्	this
उह्यते	is carried
उपक्रीय	having bought
करोमि	I do
गृहीत्वा	having grabbed
तृतीय०	third
त्रयः	three
द्वितीय०	second
धृत्वा	having put
प्रथम०	first
यज्ञच्छागः	a goat for a sacrifice
यज्ञार्थम्	for a sacrifice

Chapter 17 Exercises

Section A

Translate the following:

1. तानि वचनानि
2. तम् वृक्षम्
3. सः दुर्जनः
4. सा भार्या
5. तस्मिन् वृक्षे
6. तस्य स्कन्धेन
7. भोः राम
8. तत् पुस्तकम्
9. अन्ये नराः
10. नगरस्य समीपे

Section B

Translate the following:

1. Having heard those words
2. Having seen those boys
3. Having fallen from that mountain
4. Having run to that town
5. Having become tall
6. Having seen that fruit
7. Having eaten those fruits
8. Having walked to the town
9. Having heard him
10. Having seen those two wives

Section C

(a) Say which of the following are complete sentences;
(b) Translate each.

1. तानि वचनानि श्रुत्वा वनम् अगच्छत्।
2. ताम् दृष्ट्वा रामः
3. तत् नगरम् धावित्वा शीघ्रम्
4. सहसा बालकम् तुदित्वा सः नरः नगरात् अधावत्।
5. भार्या तम् दृष्ट्वा

Section D

Translate the following:

1. तानि वचनानि श्रुत्वा नृपस्य पुत्रः रामः नाम वनम् अगच्छत्।
2. सः नरः तत् वनम् शीघ्रम् अधावत्।
3. तस्य नरस्य भार्याम् दृष्ट्वा सीता गृहम् अचरत्।
4. तस्मिन् वने प्राज्ञाः नराः नित्यम् वसन्ति।
5. तम् अपश्यम् इति श्रुत्वा सीता शान्ता अभवत्।
6. एकदा वने वीरः नरः कृष्णम् सिंहम् अपश्यत्।
7. ताम् नौकाम् दृष्ट्वा गजः वनम् शीघ्रम् अचरत्।
8. तस्याम् पेटायाम् वीराः नराः अतिष्ठन्।
9. तेन लगुडेन तम् तुदित्वा घोरः चौरः गृहात् अधावत्।
10. तारकाः दृष्ट्वा खगः गजम् अवदत् हे गज कदा वनम् अगच्छः इति।

Section E

Translate the following into Sanskrit:

1. The wise men stand near the donkey.
2. The evil man saw that man's wife.
3. "You were running," said the horrible lady.
4. Therefore the king's son will quickly eat that food.
5. The boy led the large elephant to the town.
6. Having heard the boy's words, the thieves ran to a friend's house.
7. Having seen the lady's friend, the man went to the forest.
8. Having eaten the food, the dog stood near the wise man.
9. Having fallen from the tree, the bird quickly walked away from the horrible snake.
10. Having gone to the town by boat, the brave ladies will see the king's large house.

Section F

Translate into Sanskrit:

One day a dog went to the house of a wise man. Here the wise man was eating food. Having thought, "I will eat that food", the dog ran to the man and hit him. Having grabbed the food quickly, he ran away from the house to the forest. In the forest he ate the food. But the wise man ran after the dog. Having seen him, he stood near him and asked, "Would you like (some) fruit, Kṛṣṇa?" Suddenly Kṛṣṇa came to the man and said, "O man, you have become very wise."

Having grabbed = गृहीत्वा

18. THE MEN AND THE GOLD

I. *Vocabulary:* Learn the following words.

काञ्चनम्	gold	शरीरम्	body
पिष्टकम्	bread; cake	क्षुधित॰	hungry
दधिकम्	cheese	दधाति	places
विषम्	poison	मिलति	meets
क्लेशः	pain; grief	हन्ति	he kills

II.*Grammar*:

The Past Passive Participle:

The Past Passive Participle (PPP) is formed by replacing the त्वा of the Past Active Participle (PAP) with a त०.

Indicative	Participle		English
Present	Past Active	Past Passive	Meaning
त्यजति	त्यक्त्वा	त्यक्त०	abandoned
भवति	भूत्वा	भूत०	become
जयति	जित्वा	जित०	conquered
खादति	खादित्वा	खादित०	eaten
पतति	पतित्वा	पतित०	fallen
ददाति	दत्त्वा	दत्त०	given
गच्छति	गत्वा	गत०	gone
शृणोति	श्रुत्वा	श्रुत०	heard
हन्ति	हत्वा	हत०	killed
मिलति	मिलित्वा	मिलित०	met
रक्षति	रक्षित्वा	रक्षित०	protected
वदति	उदित्वा	उदित०	said
पश्यति	दृष्ट्वा	दृष्ट०	seen
चरति	चरित्वा	चरित०	walked

III. *Syntax*:

The Uses of the Past Passive Participle

A. The name "Past Passive Participle" given by Western Grammarians describes use of this form: it is a Participle, expressing an action which happened in the past and which affects the person or thing which it describes.

For example:

नरः हतः स्वर्गम् गच्छति। A dead man goes to heaven.

These forms have to agree like विशेषण with whatever they are describing.

In English it is often necessary to translate a Past Participle Passive with a 'who' or 'which'.

For example:

नरः तुदितः भूमिम् अपतत्।

The man, who had been hit, fell to the ground.

नारी तुदिता भूमिम् अपतत्।

The lady, who had been hit, fell to the ground.

गृहम् तुदितम् भूमिम् अपतत्।

The house, which had been hit, fell to the ground.

B. The Past Passive Participle can be used to form a whole sentence, either with or without a form of भवति.

गजः वनम् गतः। The elephant has gone to the forest.

गजः हतः भवति। The elephant becomes dead.

C. To express the Agent of the action with the Past Passive Participle the तृतीता विभक्ति is used.

For example,

तत् रामेण कृतम्। That was done by Rāma.

रामः सीतया दृष्टः। Rāma was seen by Sītā.

सीता नरेण दृष्टा। Sīta was seen by the man.

॥नराः काञ्चनम् च॥

एकदा नराः मार्गे अचरन्। प्राज्ञः नरः तैः मिलितः। हे नराः मा तत्र गच्छत। तत्र हि महान् क्लेशः भविष्यति इति तेन प्राज्ञेन नरेण उदितम्। तानि वचनानि तेन उदितानि श्रुत्वा नरैः उदितम् मा तत् वद हे नर। अभयाः हि स्मः इति। तस्मात् तस्मिन् मार्गे अचरन्। अचिरेण वृक्षस्य समीपे काञ्चनम् तैः दृष्टम्। ते क्षुधिताः भूताः। तस्मात् नरौ नगरम् अगच्छताम्। तत्र पिष्टकम् दधिजम् च खादित्वा तौ नरौ अचिन्तयताम् सर्वम् काञ्चनम् इच्छावः। यदि विषम् आहारे दध्यावः तर्हि अन्यौ हतौ भविष्यतः। विषम् मित्रयोः आहारे अदधान्। वृक्षस्य समीपे तु अन्याभ्याम् काञ्चनम् रक्षितम्। अचिन्तयताम् सर्वम् काञ्चनम् इच्छावः। तस्मात् मित्रे व्यापादिष्यावः इति। नगरात् वृक्षम् गत्वा नरौ मित्राभ्याम् हतौ। ताभ्याम् तु विषम् खादितम्। सर्वे नराः हताः अभवन्। अचिरेण प्राज्ञेन नरेण तेषाम् शरीराणि दृष्टानि। काञ्चनम् तेन दृष्टम्। समुद्रे तत् अक्षिपत्।

तर्हि	then
महान्	great (*masculine, singular)*
सर्व०	all
स्मः	we are
यदि	if

Chaper 18 Exercises

Section A

Translate the following:

1. गतः
2. खादिता
3. दृष्टः
4. तुदितः
5. श्रुतम्
6. two (men) seen
7. gone to (n.sing)
8. killed (m.pl.)
9. eaten (m.sing)
10. heard (n.pl)

Section B

Translate the following:

1. वचनम् तेन श्रुतम्।
2. सीता रामेण मिलिता।
3. रामः कुपितेन नरेण दृष्टः।
4. गजः हस्तेन तुदितः।
5. प्राज्ञस्य नरस्य वचनानि श्रुतानि।
6. तानि वचनानि तेन नरेण उदितानि।
7. पिष्टकम् तस्य भार्यया खादितम् इति सीता मित्रम् अवदत्।
8. दधिजम् वृक्षात् पतितम् नरः हस्तेन अहरत्।
9. हतम् मूषिकम् गृहे त्यक्तम् दृष्ट्वा बिडालः तम् अखादत्।
10. विषम् नरेण तस्मै दत्तम् बालकेन दृष्टम्।

Section C

Translate the following into Sanskrit:

1. That was seen by the man's wife.
2. The cheese was seen and eaten by that bird.
3. The boys will eat the fruits which have fallen from the trees.
4. The dog was hit by the man with (his) hand.
5. In the abandoned house, the boys are living.
6. Having seen that bird which had fallen from the tree, we will go to the forest.
7. The book was given by the boys to (their) father.
8. Protect that small boy who has been abandoned by (his) angry father.
9. The eldest son, Rāma by name, was seen by his friend's wife.
10. The stars were seen in the sky by the brave boys.

18A. THE CROW AND THE QUAIL

II. *Vocabulary*: Learn the following words.

वर्तकः	quail	गोपालः	herdsman
काकः	crow	कः	who?
तीरः	bank; shore	अथ	then
भाण्डः	pot	वारम् वारम्	often

II. *Revision*:

This chapter is intended for revision of the complete course, and practice in what has been studied. Therefore, nothing new is presented. The Grammar and Vocabulary Sections at the back of the book provide ample revision material to accompany the exercises.

॥वर्तकः काकः च॥

एकदा सर्वे खगाः समुद्रस्य तीरम् अगच्छन्। तत्र काकेन सह वर्तकः अगच्छत्। अथ गोपालः समुद्रस्य तीरम् मार्गेण अगच्छत्। तस्य शिरसि भाण्डः स्थितः। भाण्डे फलानि। सः काकः वारम् वारम् तानि फलानि अखादत्। नगरम् गत्वा गोपालः भाण्डम् भूमौ अदधात्। फलानि खादितानि दृष्ट्वा गोपालः अचिन्तयत् कः तानि फलानि अखादत् इति। काकम् वर्तकम् च अपश्यत्। ततः खेदितः काकः शीघ्रम् अपलायत।

वर्तकः मन्दगतिः तेन प्राप्तः व्यापादितः। अतः अहम् वदामि।

न स्थातव्यम् न गन्तव्यम् दुर्जनेन समम् क्वचित्।
काकसङ्गात् हतः हंसः तिष्ठन् गच्छन् च वर्तकः॥

अतः	therefore
अदधात्	he placed
अपलायत	he fled
खेदित०	sad
प्राप्तः व्यापादितः	was taken and killed
भूमौ	on the ground
मन्दगतिः	slow to move
शिरसि	on the head
सर्वे	all
स्थित०	placed

<u>The Final Verse</u>

'One must not stand (स्थातव्यम्) with or go (गन्तव्यम्) with (समम्) an evil person anywhere (क्वचित्). Because he was in the company of a crow (काकसङ्गात्) the swan (हंसः) was killed (हतः) as he waited (तिष्ठन्) and the quail as he was travelling (गच्छन्).'

(This verse is a quotation from the Hitopadeśa)

Chaper 18A Exercises: Revision of Parts 1 & 2

Section A

Write out all the forms of:

1. रामः	3. ज्ञानम्	5. सः
2. सीता	4. तत्	6. सा

Section B

Write out the Present, Future and Past Indicative, and the Imperative of भवति.

Section C

Give the of the Future of each of the following, with a translation.

1. पश्यति	4. गच्छति	7. भवति
2. पतति	5. वदति	8. आगच्छति
3. चरति	6. तुदति	9. धावति

Section D

Translate the following into Sanskrit:

1. Having become	3. Having run	5. Having seen
2. Having gone	4. Having hit	6. Having heard

Section E

Translate the following into Sanskrit:

1. The man was seen.
2. That was eaten by that dog.
3. Go to that man now, boy!
4. Do not run from the forest to the house seen by the peaceful wife, men.
5. Do not let the large army go to the house seen by the messengers from that father's house.

Section F

Translate the following into Sanskrit:

One day a man was walking in the forest. Having seen a large lion, he thought, 'Where will I go? The lion will eat me.' Then a tall tree was seen by him. Having run to the tree, he saw a man. That man was standing near it. The man was carrying a stick. 'I will hit the lion with that stick. Then he will run away from the forest,' thought the man. Therefore he said to the man, 'A lion is standing near that tree.' Having heard this, the second man quickly ran away. Therefore the first man, having grabbed the stick, struck the lion. The lion was killed by that man with the stick.

me	माम्
first	प्रथम०
second	द्वितीय०
was killed	हत०

A. SUMMARY OF GRAMMAR

रामः

रामः	रामौ	रामाः
हे राम	हे रामौ	हे रामाः
रामम्	रामौ	रामान्
रामेण	रामाभ्याम्	रामैः
रामाय	रामाभ्याम्	रामेभ्यः
रामात्	रामाभ्याम्	रामेभ्यः
रामस्य	रामयोः	रामाणाम्
रामे	रामयोः	रामेषु

ज्ञानम्

ज्ञानम्	ज्ञाने	ज्ञानानि
हे ज्ञान	हे ज्ञाने	हे ज्ञानानि
ज्ञानम्	ज्ञाने	ज्ञानानि
ज्ञानेन	ज्ञानाभ्याम्	ज्ञानैः
ज्ञानाय	ज्ञानाभ्याम्	ज्ञानेभ्यः
ज्ञानात्	ज्ञानाभ्याम्	ज्ञानेभ्यः
ज्ञानस्य	ज्ञानयोः	ज्ञानानाम्
ज्ञाने	ज्ञानयोः	ज्ञानेषु

सीता

सीता	सीते	सीताः
हे सीते	हे सीते	हे सीताः
सीताम्	सीते	सीताः
सीतया	सीताभ्याम्	सीताभिः
सीतायै	सीताभ्याम्	सीताभ्यः
सीतायाः	सीताभ्याम्	सीताभ्यः
सीतायाः	सीतयोः	सीतानाम्
सीतायाम्	सीतयोः	सीतासु

The Forms of विशेषण

पुंलिङ्ग			स्त्रीलिङ्ग			नपुंसकलिङ्ग		
शान्तः	शान्तौ	शान्ताः	शान्ता	शान्ते	शान्ताः	शान्तम्	शान्ते	शान्तानि
शान्त	शान्तौ	शान्ताः	शान्ते	शान्ते	शान्ताः	शान्त	शान्ते	शान्तानि
शान्तम्	शान्तौ	शान्तान्	शान्ताम्	शान्ते	शान्ताः	शान्तम्	शान्ते	शान्तानि
शान्तेन	शान्ताभ्याम्	शान्तैः	शान्तया	शान्ताभ्याम्	शान्ताभिः	शान्तेन	शान्ताभ्याम्	शान्तैः
शान्ताय	शान्ताभ्याम्	शान्तेभ्यः	शान्तायै	शान्ताभ्याम्	शान्ताभ्यः	शान्ताय	शान्ताभ्याम्	शान्तेभ्यः
शान्तात्	शान्ताभ्याम्	शान्तेभ्यः	शान्तायाः	शान्ताभ्याम्	शान्ताभ्यः	शान्तात्	शान्ताभ्याम्	शान्तेभ्यः
शान्तस्य	शान्तयोः	शान्तानाम्	शान्तायाः	शान्तयोः	शान्तानाम्	शान्तस्य	शान्तयोः	शान्तानाम्
शान्ते	शान्तयोः	शान्तेषु	शान्तायाम्	शान्तयोः	शान्तासु	शान्ते	शान्तयोः	शान्तेषु

The Forms of तत्

पुंलिङ्ग			स्त्रीलिङ्ग			नपुंसकलिङ्ग		
सः	तौ	ते	सा	ते	ताः	तत्	ते	तानि
तम्	तौ	तान्	ताम्	ते	ताः	तत्	ते	तानि
तेन	ताभ्याम्	तैः	तया	ताभ्याम्	ताभिः	तेन	ताभ्याम्	तैः
तस्मै	ताभ्याम्	तेभ्यः	तस्यै	ताभ्याम्	ताभ्यः	तस्मै	ताभ्याम्	तेभ्यः
तस्मात्	ताभ्याम्	तेभ्यः	तस्याः	ताभ्याम्	ताभ्यः	तस्मात्	ताभ्याम्	तेभ्यः
तस्य	तयोः	तेषाम्	तस्याः	तयोः	तासाम्	तस्य	तयोः	तेषाम्
तस्मिन्	तयोः	तेषु	तस्याम्	तयोः	तासु	तस्मिन्	तयोः	तेषु

क्रिया Present, Future and Past

Present

भवति	भवतः	भवन्ति
भवसि	भवथः	भवथ
भवामि	भवावः	भवामः

Future

भविष्यति	भविष्यतः	भविष्यन्ति
भविष्यसि	भविष्यथः	भविष्यथ
भविष्यामि	भविष्यावः	भविष्यामः

Past

अभवत्	अभवताम्	अभवन्
अभवः	अभवतम्	अभवत
अभवम्	अभवाव	अभवाम

The Imperative - लोट्

भवतु	भवताम्	भवन्तु
भव	भवतम्	भवत
भवानि	भवाव	भवाम

Future

Present	Meaning	Future	Meaning
वदति	says	वदिष्यति	will say
पतति	falls	पतिष्यति	will fall
चरति	walks	चरिष्यति	will walk
तुदति	hits	तोत्स्यति	will hit
चिन्तयति	thinks	चिन्तयिष्यति	will think
धावति	runs	धाविष्यति	will run
भवति	becomes	भविष्यति	will become
गच्छति	goes	गमिष्यति	will go
आगच्छति	comes	आगमिष्यति	will come
जीवति	lives	जीविष्यति	will live
ददाति	gives	दास्यति	will give
शृणोति	hears	श्रोष्यति	will hear
पश्यति	sees	द्रक्ष्यति	will see

Past

Present	Meaning	Past	Meaning
वदति	says	अवदत्	said
पतति	falls	अपतत्	fell
चरति	walks	अचरत्	walked
पश्यति	sees	अपश्यत्	saw
तुदति	hits	अतुदत्	hit
चिन्तयति	thinks	अचिन्तयत्	thought
धावति	runs	अधावत्	ran
गच्छति	goes	अगच्छत्	went
आगच्छति	comes	आगच्छत्	came

Past Participles

Indicative	Participles			
Present	Active	Meaning	Passive	Meaning
त्यजति	त्यक्त्वा	having abandoned	त्यक्त०	abandoned
भवति	भूत्वा	having become	भूत०	become
जयति	जित्वा	having conquered	जित०	conquered
खादति	खादित्वा	having eaten	खादित०	eaten
पतति	पतित्वा	having fallen	पतित०	fallen
ददाति	दत्त्वा	having given	दत्त०	given
गच्छति	गत्वा	having gone	गत०	gone
शृणोति	श्रुत्वा	having heard	श्रुत०	heard
वदति	उदित्वा	having said	उदित०	said
पश्यति	दृष्ट्वा	having seen	दृष्ट०	seen
चरति	चरित्वा	having walked	चरित०	walked

Complete List of Verbal Formations

Meaning	Present	Future	Imperfect	PAP	PPP
becomes	भवति	भविष्यति	अभवत्	भूत्वा	भूत॰
burns	दहति	धक्ष्यति	अदहत्	दग्ध्वा	दग्ध॰
carries	हरति	हरिष्यति	अहरत्	हृत्वा	हृत॰
comes	आगच्छति	आगमिष्यति	आगच्छत्	आगम्य	आगत॰
eats	खादति	खादिष्यति	अखादत्	खादित्वा	खादित॰
falls	पतति	पतिष्यति	अपतत्	पतित्वा	पतित॰
gives	ददाति	दास्यति	अददात्	दत्त्वा	दत्त॰
goes	गच्छति	गमिष्यति	अगच्छत्	गत्वा	गत॰
hears	शृणोति	श्रोष्यति	अशृणोत्	श्रुत्वा	श्रुत॰
hits	तुदति	तोत्स्यति	अतुदत्	तुदित्वा	तुदित॰
kills	हन्ति	हनिष्यति	अहन्	हत्वा	हत॰
leaves	त्यजति	त्यक्ष्यति	अत्यजत्	त्यक्त्वा	त्यक्त॰
lives	जीवति	जीविष्यति	अजीवत्	जीवित्वा	जीवित॰
runs	धावति	धाविष्यति	अधावत्	धावित्वा	धावित॰
says	वदति	वदिष्यति	अवदत्	उदित्वा	उदित॰
sees	पश्यति	द्रक्ष्यति	अपश्यत्	दृष्ट्वा	दृष्ट॰
thinks	चिन्तयति	चिन्तयिष्यति	अचिन्तयत्	चिन्तयित्वा	चिन्तयित॰
walks	चरति	चरिष्यति	अचरत्	चरित्वा	चरित॰

B. SUMMARY OF SYNTAX

The Use of the विभक्ति

विभक्ति	Question Answered	Example (Meaning)	
प्रथमा विभक्ति Nominative	who? (Subject)	रामः	Rāma
संबोधन Vocative	who is called?	हे राम	O Rāma
द्वितीया विभक्ति Accusative	what? (Object)	रामम्	Rāma
तृतीया विभक्ति Instrumental	by/with what?	रामेण	by/with Rāma
चतुर्थी विभक्ति Dative	for whom?	रामाय	to/for Rāma
पञ्चमी विभक्ति Ablative	from whom?	रामात्	from Rāma
षष्ठी विभक्ति Genitive	whose?	रामस्य	of Rāma
सप्तमी विभक्ति Locative	where?	रामे	in Rāma

The विभक्ति Rules

The प्रथमा विभक्ति Rule

The प्रथमा विभक्ति shows the Subject of a Sentence.

The संबोधन Rule

The संबोधन shows who is being called.

The द्वितीया विभक्ति Rule

The द्वितीया विभक्ति shows the Object of an action.

The तृतीया विभक्ति Rule

The तृतीया विभक्ति shows by or with what an action is done.

The चतुर्थी विभक्ति Rule

The चतुर्थी विभक्ति shows to whom something is offered.

The पञ्चमी विभक्ति Rule

The पञ्चमी विभक्ति shows from where something comes.

The षष्ठी विभक्ति Rule

The षष्ठी विभक्ति shows who has something.

The सप्तमी विभक्ति Rule

The सप्तमी विभक्ति shows where an action happens.

C. SANSKRIT-ENGLISH VOCABULARY

अचलः	mountain	इति	*end of speech*
अचिरेण	soon	इदानीम्	now
अतीव	very	उत्तम०	best
अत्र	here	उन्नत०	tall
अथ	then	एकदा	one day
अनन्तरम्	immediately	कः	who?
अनेक०	many	कदा	when?
अन्य०	(an)other	कथयति	tells
अभय०	fearless	कथा	story
अरुण०	red	कथम्	how?
अल्प०	small	काकः	crow
अश्वः	horse	काञ्चनम्	gold
अहम्	I	किम्	what?
आगच्छति	comes	किमिति	why?
आनयति	brings	किंतु	but
आश्रमः	hermitage	कुक्कुरः	dog
आस्यम्	mouth	कुतः	why?
आहारः	food	कुत्र	where?
इच्छति	wants	कुपित०	angry

कृष्ण०	black	चरित्रम्	adventure
केशः	hair	चिन्तयति	thinks
क्रोशति	cries out	चिरेण	after a while
क्लेशः	pain; grief	चौरः	thief
क्षिपति	throws; shoots	छागः	goat
क्षुधित०	hungry	जनकः	father
खगः	bird	जयति	conquers
खड्गः	sword	जलम्	water
खादति	eats	जानाति	knows
गगनम्	sky	ज्ञानम्	knowledge
गच्छति	goes	जीवति	lives
गजः	elephant	ज्येष्ठ०	eldest
गमिष्यति	will go	तत्र	there
गर्दभः	donkey	तरति	crosses over
गायति	sings	तस्मात्	therefore
गृहम्	house	तारका	star
गोविन्दः	Govinda	तिष्ठति	stands
गोपालः	farmer	तीरः	bank
घोरः	horrible	तु	but
च	and	तुदति	hits; strikes
चरति	walks	त्यजति	abandons; leaves

ददाति	gives
दधाति	places
दधिजम्	cheese
दहति	burns
दर्शयति	shows
दीर्घ०	long
दुर्जनः	evil person
दुर्बल०	weak
दूतः	messenger
देहः	body
द्रक्ष्यति	will see
द्वीपः	island
धावति	runs
न	not
नगरम्	town; city
नयति	leads
नरः	man
नादः	roar
नाम	named
नासिका	nose
नित्यम्	always
नृपः	king
नौका	boat
पतति	falls
पादः	foot
पिबति	drinks
पीठम्	chair
पुत्रः	son
पुनः	again
पुष्पम्	flower
पुस्तकम्	book
पृच्छति	asks
पेटा	box
प्रबल०	strong
प्राज्ञ०	wise
प्रिय०	dear
फलम्	fruit
बहुकालम्	for a long time
बध्नाति	binds
बालकः	boy
बिडालः	cat
ब्राह्मणः	Brāhmaṇa

भयम्	fear
भवति	becomes
भागः	part; portion
भाण्डः	pot
भार्या	wife
भोः	O!
मत्स्यः	fish
मार्गः	path; road
मित्रम्	friend
मिलति	meets
मूषिकः	mouse
मृगः	deer
मेषः	sheep
यज्ञः	sacrifice
रक्षति	protects
रथः	chariot
लगुडः	stick
लोकः	world
वचनम्	command; statement; word
वदति	says
वनम्	forest
वन्दनम्	thank you
वरम्	boon
वर्तकः	quail
वर्षः	year
वसति	dwells
वारम् वारम्	often
विषम्	poison
वीर०	brave
वृक्षः	tree
व्याघ्रः	tiger
व्यापादयति	kills

शब्दः	sound
शय्या	bed
शशकः	rabbit
शान्त०	peaceful
शाला	room
शीघ्रम्	quickly
शुद्ध०	pure
शृणोति	hears
श्रेष्ठ०	best
श्रोष्यति	will hear
सत्यम्	truth
समीपे	near (+Gen.)
समुद्रः	ocean; sea
सन्तुष्ट०	contented
सर्पः	snake
सह	together with (after Instr.)
सहसा	suddenly
सिंहः	lion
सूर्यः	sun
सेना	army
स्कन्धः	shoulder
स्वर्गः	heaven
स्पृशति	touches
हरति	grabs
हस्तः	hand

D. ENGLISH-SANSKRIT VOCABULARY

abandons	त्यजति
adventure	चरित्रम्
after a while	चिरेण
again	पुनः
always	नित्यम्
and	च
angry	कुपित०
another	अन्य०
army	सेना
asks	पृच्छति
bank	तीरः
becomes	भवति
bed	शय्या
best	उत्तम० श्रेष्ठ०
binds	बध्नाति
bird	खगः
black	कृष्ण०
boat	नौका
body	देहः
book	पुस्तकम्
boon	वरम्
box	पेटा
boy	बालकः
Brāhmaṇa	ब्राह्मणः
brave	वीर०
bread	पिष्टकम्
brings	आनयति
burns	दहति
but	किंतु तु
cat	बिडालः
chair	पीठम्
chariot	रथः
cheese	दधिकम्
city	नगरम्
comes	आगच्छति
command	वचनम्
conquers	जयति
contented	सन्तुष्ट०
cries out	क्रोशति
crosses over	तरति

crow	काकः	forest	वनम्
dear	प्रिय०	friend	मित्रम्
deer	मृगः	fruit	फलम्
dog	कुक्कुरः	gives	ददाति
donkey	गर्दभः	goat	छागः
drinks	पिबति	goes	गच्छति
dwells	वसति	gold	काञ्चनम्
eats	खादति	Govinda	गोविन्दः
eldest	ज्येष्ठ०	grabs	हरति
elephant	गजः	grief	क्लेशः
evil person	दुर्जनः	hair	केशः
falls	पतति	hand	हस्तः
farmer	गोपालः	hears	शृणोति
father	जनकः	heaven	स्वर्गः
fear	भयम्	here	अत्र
fearless	अभय०	hermitage	आश्रमः
fish	मत्स्यः	hits	तुदति
flower	पुष्पम्	horrible	घोरः
food	आहारः	horse	अश्वः
foot	पादः	house	गृहम्
for a long time	बहुकालम्	how?	कथम्

I	अहम्
immediately	अनन्तरम्
island	द्वीपः
kills	व्यापादयति
king	नृपः
knowledge	ज्ञानम्
knows	जानाति
leads	नयति
leaves	त्यजति
lion	सिंहः
lives	जीवति
long	दीर्घ०
man	नरः
many	अनेक०
meets	मिलति
messenger	दूतः
mountain	अचलः
mouse	मूषिकः
mouth	आस्यम्
named	नाम
near (with 6th)	समीपे

nose	नासिका
not	न
now	इदानीम्
O!	भोः
ocean	समुद्रः
often	वारम् वारम्
one day	एकदा
other	अन्य०
part	भागः
path	मार्गः
peaceful	शान्त०
places	दधाति
poison	विषम्
portion	भागः
pot	भाण्डः
protects	रक्षति
pure	शुद्ध०
quail	वर्तकः
quickly	शीघ्रम्
rabbit	शशकः
red	अरूण०

road	मार्गः
roar	नादः
room	शाला
runs	धावति
sacrifice	यज्ञः
says	वदति
sea	समुद्रः
sheep	मेषः
shoots	क्षिपति
shoulder	स्कन्धः
shows	दर्शयति
sings	गायति
sky	गगनम्
small	अल्प०
snake	सर्पः
son	पुत्रः
soon	अचिरेण
sound	शब्दः
stands	तिष्ठति
star	तारका
statement	वचनम्
stick	लगुडः
story	कथा
strikes	तुदति
strong	प्रबल०
suddenly	सहसा
sun	सूर्यः
sword	खड्गः
tall	उन्नत०
tells	कथयति
thank you	वन्दनम्
then	अथ
there	तत्र
therefore	तस्मात्
thief	चौरः
thinks	चिन्तयति
throws	क्षिपति
tiger	व्याघ्रः
together with (after Instru.)	सह
touches	स्पृशति
town	नगरम्
tree	वृक्षः

truth	सत्यम्	why?	कुतः किमिति
very	अतीव	wife	भार्या
walks	चरति	will go	गमिष्यति
wants	इच्छति	will hear	श्रोष्यति
water	जलम्	will see	द्रक्ष्यति
weak	दुर्बल०	wise	प्राज्ञ०
what?	किम्	word	वचनम्
when?	कदा	world	लोकः
where?	कुत्र	year	वर्षः
who?	कः		